THE ORGANIZATION AND ADMINISTRATION OF HIGHER EDUCATION IN INDIA SINCE INDEPENDENCE

N. Koshy Samuel

UNIVERSITY
PRESS OF
AMERICA

DEDICATION

To my wife and children.

TABLE OF CONTENTS

v

vi

LIST OF TABLES

LIST OF ILLUSTRATIONS

December 20, 1982

FOREWORD

The educational system in India is a subject of some relevance to people in the United States of America. It is out of this system that the thousands of Indian professionals in the United States - teachers, doctors, engineers, scientists and technologists- have emerged and managed to merge into the stream of American life and society. The intellectual relationship between India and the United States is a product of the human values and liberal freedoms underlying the educational system in our two countries and animating the two great democracies of the world. By bringing out this book, Dr.Koshy Samuel has made a contribution not only to the understanding of the Indian system of education but of the basic aims, objectives and aspirations of India since independence.

Dr.Samuel's study is a comprehensive one. Beginning with a brief historical background, it covers the role of higher education and the salient aspects of the organization and administration of higher education in India since independence, and finally the educational system as a whole. The book traces the process of the gradual transformation of education from a colonially oriented one into a national system geared to the needs and requirements of an independent nation engaged in developing and changing an ancient society into a modern one at the same time holding on to the basic values of our age-old culture and civilization.

India,being a developing country of 700 million people, has naturally placed primary emphasis on elementary, second-secondary, higher-secondary education. However, higher education is encouraged to the maximum extent possible. We believe that in a rapidly changing world, where knowledge is advancing by leaps and bounds, it is necessary for a developing country to have peaks of educational progress together with progress in mass education if we are to be in a position to lift the entire people to a higher educational level and be on a par with the rest of the world. It is as a result of this policy that we have today in India a sizeable cross-section of educated people including the third largest pool of scientific and technical personnel after the United States and the Soviet Union. These are major achievements, but there are also many difficulties and short-comings to be overcome. Dr.Samuel has dealt with both making this book an important addition to the literature on higher education in India.

(K.R.Narayanan)

PREFACE

India attained independence on August 15, 1947, as a dominion of the British Commonwealth of Nations, and it elected to become an independent republic in 1950. With the birth of independent India came a host of problems, among which was the problem of higher education.

Prior to independence, the structure of education in India varied from state to state. University education had two stages: a two-year intermediate stage and a two-year degree stage. The medium of instruction was English. The curriculum in secondary schools was academic in character in order to meet the requirements of university education. For the majority of high school students, secondary education was the terminal stage. On the whole, the system of education was neither national in character nor fully adequate in terms of size and quality. Moreover, higher education in India was not geared to the country's needs. It was controlled and geared into the English structure.

Today, more than ever before, there is a nationwide emphasis on higher education in India. This is observed in the marked expansion of higher educational institutions. In 35 years the arts and sciences colleges have increased from 500 to 4,558. While there were only 19 universities in 1947, now there are 137. A map of India showing the distribution of universities is given in Appendix A.

After independence, there was a keen desire to revise the higher educational system of India, and to introduce the liberal and scientific ideas of institutions of higher learning. The time has now come in Indian educational history to lay a great emphasis on quality. India is undergoing constant change and it will be interesting and helpful to analyze the changing role and progress of Indian institutions of higher learning.

In this book, an attempt has been made to examine the present role as well as the future needs of higher education in India. The major purpose of this book is to analyze the administration and organizational structure of Indian institutions of higher learning after independence.

xv

A minor objective is to include a brief sketch of the historical development of higher education in the Hindu, Buddhist, Medieval, and British periods. A section has been devoted to the general aims and functions of higher education, and the role of the state and central governments in the field of higher education.

This book consists of a descriptive and analytical study of the administration and organization of higher education in India since independence. Quantitative aspects of growth and enrollment in the institutions of higher learning, as well as curricular expansion, and qualitative aspects, were also analyzed.

A review of literature relating to Indian higher education, expecially the development of higher education since independence, was done. The Indian Embassy, the Library of Congress, the United States Office of Education, and many other libraries provided valuable information needed for this paper. Government documents, official documents of commissions, annual reports, handbooks, historical works, pamphlets, and periodicals were the various sources used for necessary material.

Comparative studies on the development of higher education in India after independence are limited. However, a few descriptive studies and dissertations have been done on various aspects of higher education both before and after independence.

CHAPTER I

HISTORICAL DEVELOPMENT OF HIGHER EDUCATION

To appreciate and understand the role of higher education in India since independence, it is necessary to have some knowledge of its historical development. Hence, the purpose of this chapter is to present a brief historical development of higher education in India from the earliest times until the end of the British period in 1947. This period of pre-independence may be divided into four phases: (1) the ancient Hindu period, prior to the sixth century B.C.; (2) the Buddhist times, sixth century B.C. to tenth century A.D.; (3) Medieval times—the Muslim rule, tenth to eighteenth century A.D.; and (4) British India, 1780 to 1947.

The Ancient Hindu Period

The history of universities in India dates back to the days of antiquity. Not much is known about the educational conditions before the advent of Aryans, so we cannot definitely say whether there were institutions similar to the modern universities. However, there is ample evidence to show "that the ancient Aryans had a well developed system of higher education and that the institutions which imparted such education are comparable to some extent to the colleges and universities of today."[1]

From the earliest times, India has known the university and its function. It is believed by some scholars that "even before the arrival of the Aryans, there were universities of some type, though not of the modern nature."[2]

Haggerty gives an overview of ancient systems of Indian education. He states that several types of higher education centres existed in ancient India. "One consisted of a single teacher, or guru, who instructed his pupils in a particular Veda or in a subject such as grammar or logic. Another was run by legally constituted assemblies of scholars who were specialists in the Vedas and Dharma Sutras."[3] These assemblies may have been the forerunners of the later Brahmanic universities, the most important and famous of which

1

were in Taksasila (Taxila) and Nalanda. Brahmanic universities originated in the 7th century B.C. and flourished for almost 1,000 years. They had highly developed curriculums in several areas such as astrology, astronomy, medicine, surgery, and Vedic philosophy; and enrolled as many as 10,000 students, for their fame attracted students from nearby countries. For example, Fa Hien and Hiuen Tsang of China have recorded much about the organization and course of instruction in Taksasila and Nalanda.[4]

Dongerkery gives a parallel thought concerning the ancient universities:

> The ancient Indian universities
> can be traced back to the 7th
> century B.C. Takshasila, Nalanda,
> Vikramsila, Valabhi, Banaras and
> Kanchi are names to conjure with.
> The names of Nagarjuna, Vasuban-
> dhum Dinnaga, Sthiramathi, Darma-
> pala Santaraksita, and Atisa,
> to mention only a few, will be
> remembered for their learning
> and scholarship as long as great
> teachers and scholars in seats
> of learning continue to be honoured
> and respected in his country.
> The international reputation attained
> by some of these universities
> and their teachers attracted stu-
> dents and scholars not only from
> distant parts of India but also
> from Tibet, China, Ceylon and Korea.[5]

Though the universities of modern India owe very little to our ancient centres of learning, one must not forget the existence of such centres since very early times. Regarding it, the report of the University Education Commission states:

> The parishads or assemblies of
> Brahmans learned in the Vedas
> and Dharma Sutras probably attracted
> a number of students desirous
> of acquiring knowledge like Sveta-
> ketu in the Chandogya Upanishad.
> Later there grew up well organized
> centres of learning of which the

2

most famous were Takshasila and
Nalanda. One of the Jatakas re-
lates the story of the sixteen
year old son of the king of Banaras
who went to distant Takshasila
with a thousand pieces of gold,
the fee for this teacher who was
to take him through the various
branches of learning. The curriculum
at Takshasila appears to have
included the Vedas and the Vedangas
and also the eighteen arts which
comprised medicine and surgery,
astronomy and astrology, agriculture
and accouptancy, archery and snake
charming.[6]

In ancient India, they had a systematic educational system and great institutions of higher learning.
There were mainly seven higher educational centres:
Takshasila, Banaras, Nalanda, Valabhi, Kanchi, Vik-
ramshila, and Navadipa or Nadia. Also they had well
balanced curriculum in several fields such as philosophy,
astrology, astronomy, medicine, surgery and law.
Anathnath Basu describes the characteristics of the
ancient educational institution. He points out that
the characteristic educational institution of the
ancient period was the Gurukula. The Gurukulas catered
to the intellectual and educational needs of the
ancient Indian people. There the students studied
the Vedas, the rituals, literature, astronomy, medicine
and other subjects. The curriculum embraced all the
fields of intellectual activity including such subjects
as archery and principles of warfare. Though religion
occupied a large place in the curriculum, it was by
no means the only subject for study.[7]

In ancient India, education was fostered by the
state and its influence was widespread. "There existed
a network of educational institutions, hermitage schools,
monasteries, guild schools, academies and universities."[8]

The primary object of ancient education was to
teach religion. The teacher had to teach his students
how to pray, how to offer sacrifice, how to perform
their duties according to their stage in life. Besides
religious education, they were taught grammar, general
education, simple mathematics, mythology, and astrology.
So early ancient education was essentially religious
and personal.[9]

3

Regarding the contributions of the ancient Hindu period, Cramer, Browne, and Spalding state: "The country has made great contributions to the world's store of learning, particularly in mathematics, philosophy, religion, and art. . . ."[10]

The Buddhist Period

As it has been stated before, the Buddhist period was from the sixth century B.C. to the tenth century A.D. With the dawn of Buddhism in the sixth century B.C. the institutions of higher learning improved greatly. During this period the Brahmanic (Hindu) traditions of higher education were not only maintained bud also extended. Basu writes regarding this period of higher learning:

> Thus the Viharas of the Buddhist
> period became models of the Gurukulas
> of the earlier period. The Gurukulas
> continued their existence and
> received the patronage of the
> orthodox community; but as the
> religion of Buddha spread far
> and wide, the Viharas became more
> and more numerous, and they sup-
> planted the Gurukulas to some
> extent. The whole country was
> studded with them and they catered
> to the education of sections of
> the people who came under the
> influence of Buddhism.[11]

The democratic character of Buddhist education and of the Viharas has already been noted. The Viharas introduced a new element in the field of education and it brought out their similarity to modern insti-tutions more prominently. Since each Vihara was an assembly of teachers, it could organize education on a wider and more liberal basis. In this respect they were more akin to the modern colleges than the Gurukulas. Some of these Viharas were more than col-leges; in the number of students and teachers and subjects studied, they resembled the universities of our times. For example, the curriculum paralleled the European trivium (grammar, logic, and rhetoric) and quadrivium (arithmetic, astronomy, geometry and music).

4

Education in the ancient period was mainly the
education of the Vedas which consisted in the perfect
acquirement of the texts through oral repetition from
a guru or a teacher. But the Buddhist education was
not based on Vedic study. The Viharas became the
centres of learning. Takshasila, Nalanda, Valabhi
and Kanchi developed into the main centres of higher
learning. The University of Nalanda was located in
a splendid building, had a good library and an obser-
vatory. Scholars from Korea, Japan, Ceylon, Java and
Sumatra came there for studies.[12]

There were several universities scattered over
the country: The universities of Purushapura (modern
Peshawar), Takshasila (in the Punjab), Jayendra Vihara
(in Kashmir), Vikramashila Jagaddala and Odantapuri
(in Bengal), Nalanda (in Bihar), Tamralipati (in Bengal),
Kanchipura (in Madras), Valabhi (in modern Kathiavad)
and some in other places. The curriculum at Nalanda
included not only the Buddhist Scriptures but also
the Vedas, the Brahmanic literature, grammar, logic,
medicine and other subjects.[13]

From the above passage, it is evident that the
Buddhists had established a system of higher education
providing advanced curriculums in the field of religion,
literature, grammar, logic, medicine and other subjects.
Thus in the Buddhist period, Higher education advanced
greatly.

Medieval Times (The Mohammedan Period)

This section dealt with higher education in India
and its development under the Mohammedan rule. The
Mohammedan conquest of India and gradual establishment of the Mohammedan power was a setback for both
the ancient Hindu and the Buddhist learning in India.
This period covered from the tenth to the eighteenth
century A.D.

In the early centuries of Mohammedan rule many
centres of ancient and Buddhist learning were destroyed.
But as the Mohammedan empires and kingdoms were founded,
educational institutions were founded under the patronage of the Mohammedan rulers and princes. Some of
them even extended their patronage to Hindu learning.
During the Mohammedan rule various educational institutions of higher learning developed. There they
taught Mohammedan culture and learning. The more

important seats of Mohammedan power had their Madrasahs
or colleges.

The Madrasahs or Delhi, Agra, Lucknow, Rampur,
Ajmer, and Patna were famous seats of Mohammedan learning. Jaunpar in U.P. was a well known educational
centre. The college at Bidar in the South also attained
prominence in the fifteenth century. There were also
many colleges attached to the more famous of the mosques
and tombs which have served as educational centres
even from the earliest period of Mohammedan history.[14]

With the advent of Muslim rule, the institutions
of "Maktab" and "Madrasahs" were opened. A Maktab
was a primary school connected to a mosque where religion and the Koran were taught. A Madrasah was
a school of higher learning, where higher education
in science, philosophy, and law, was imparted.[15]

At the same time, some of the ancient and Buddhist
centres of learning in the east and south continued
their work throughout the middle ages. But the Mohammedan
rulers encouraged the establishment of colleges (Madrasahs)
throughout the country. The report of the University
Education Commission stated the following about the
colleges and their curriculums:

> The Mohammedan rulers encouraged
> the establishment of colleges
> (Madrasahs) at places like Lahor,
> Delhi, Rampur, Lucknow, Allahabad,
> Jaunpur, Ajmer and Bihar. Sher
> Shah who later became emperor
> was a student at Jaunpur, and
> among the subjects he studied
> there were history and philosophy,
> Arabic and Persian literature.
> The curriculum of these colleges
> paralleled the trivium and quadrivium
> of the European institutions and
> included grammar, rhetoric, logic
> and law, geometry and astronomy,
> natural philosophy, metaphysics
> and theology while poetry was
> a source of pleasure to all.
> Most of the important institutions
> attempted to specialize in one
> or more branches of knowledge

as Rampur did in logic and medicine,
Lucknow in theology and Lahore
in astronomy and mathematics.
The medium of instruction was
mainly Arabic and there were many
famous scholars in Arabic, teaching
in the institutions of higher
learning. While most of these
institutions have disappeared,
some still carry on the traditions
of the old Madrasahs.[16]

By the 11th century A.D., Madrasahs or colleges
had developed into higher educational institutions
with a distinctly religious bias. There were primarily
theological institutions, which provided instruction
in languages and other secular subjects, and were
supported or aided by the government of the day.
"The courses of instruction in the Madrasahs included
grammar, logic, theology, metaphysics, literature,
jurisprudence and science. Some of the Madrasahs
enjoyed the status of universities."[17]

In the medieval period, the education was not
for all the people of the country. It was geared
to the elite or the noble. Among the higher classes,
each pupil had a teacher all to himself. Even other
teachers had a small group of ten or twelve. Education
was a personal and family-like process. The teacher
had to live with the pupils, eating, talking, listening,
observing, encouraging and praising, scolding and
punishing them.[18] This was the same practice used
in the ancient Hindu and Buddhist periods. Humayun
Kabir, former Secretary to the Government of India
in the Ministry of Education, further states:

In the Middle ages, Muslim rulers
brought to India their own system
of education shaped under the
influence of the traditions of
Arabia and Persia. Early Islam
was revolutionary, and democratic.
In consequence, this new system
was democratic in theory. In
practice it also was confined
to a small section of the people.
There were no barriers based on
birth, but the duration of the

7

course was so long and the syllabus
so difficult as to dissuade all
except only a handful of devoted
pupils. Like ancient Indian education, this system also soon
became authoritarian and dogmatic.
What was more unfortunate was
that it developed independently
of and almost in opposition to
the indigenous Indian system.
If the two systems had established
points of contact, their distinct
dogmatisms may have led each to
modify its own dogmas, but they
continued like parallel lines
that never meet.[19]

' In the higher schools the medium of instruction
was Persian. but Arabic was obligatory for all Muslims.
Besides studying languages, they had a well balanced
program of study. The Cyclopedia of Education points
out that in the higher schools, which were supported
by imperial grants and private bounty, learned Mo-
hammedans taught Arabic, the sacred language of the
royal circle and of the court of law, where Muslim
rule was established. Besides the study of language,
rhetoric, logic, literature, law, and crude science
were taught. All students were welcome, and the Persian
schools became a common meeting ground for Hindu and
Muslim youths.[20]

The British Period

This period extended from 1708 to 1947. This
section presented a brief history of the western education in India through the various East India Com-
panies, such as Portugese, Danish, Dutch, and English,
and the movement of Christian missionaries. They
all contributed towards the introduction of western
education to India. Along the same lines, Lewis
Jennings Larson stated:

> The Portuguese under Vasco de Gaama
> arrived in Malabar, South India,
> in the last decade of the fifteenth
> century, but because they had
> trouble with Muslim traders in

8

Calicut, they moved south to Cochin and Travancore about 1500 A.D. The representatives of the Roman Catholic Church accompanied the traders. The educational contributions of the Christian bodies have exerted a major influence upon modern educational development in India.[21]

The real western or modern system of higher education started during the British period. But the histories of education reveal that Christian missionaries were active in the Indian educational field even before the arrival of the British in India. Dongerkery, in his work dealing with university education in the modern period, states that it would not be inaccurate to trace the beginning of modern education in India to the Christian missionaries who were pioneers in establishing printing presses, schools and other educational institutions in the country. Their aim was naturally directed to using education, not as an end in itself, but as a means to evangelization.[22]

Thus the beginning of the present system of education in India can be traced back to the efforts of the Christian missionaries who came to the country in the wake of European traders. With the advent of the Portuguese in the fifteenth and sixteenth centuries the Roman Catholic missionaries settled down in the different Portuguese trade settlements, mostly on the western coast of India. They started a new system of education. It consisted of theological seminaries for the training of missionaries and parochial schools for both Portuguese and Eurasian children as well as the children of the Indian Christians. Such a growth of institutions of higher learning modeled after the English style not only on the western coast of India but also in Bombay, in the Decan, and the northwest, brought about a desire for a university-type of education in the English sense. This resulted in the establishment of three universities in 1857 by law. Thus India's modern pattern of higher education began to take shape along the lines of the University of London. About the establishment of these modern universities, Siqueira stated, "Another great milestone in Indian education was laid by the

9

establishment of three universities in Culcutta, Madras, and Bombay in 1857."[23]

These three affiliating universities in Bombay, Calcutta, and Madras brought modern Indian university education into formal and legal existence. Affiliating universities are primarily an examining authority, with actual instruction offered only in the colleges that it affiliates. Most of the universities established after 1857 followed this pattern. It greatly influenced the development of higher education.[24]

The western system of education was introduced by the British, and their immediate aim was to create a class of lower administrative personnel to work with them. There was no higher education in the Indian language and even primary education was neglected. "At no time during the British reign did literacy exceed 15 percent. Facilities for technical and vocational education and research were also extremely limited."[25]

Regarding the British system of education, Cramer, Browne, and Spalding pointed out:

> In the early part of the nineteenth century the British began to encourage the organization of schools which would teach the English curriculum. This was offered as a means of permitting an intellectual elite to take over minor administrative positions, and it was hoped that its influence would work from the top downwards. The result was the training, in English, of many capable clerks **and aspirants for government positions,** but the great mass of the people was left untouched.[26]

The coming of the British brought a new system of education. They did not try to make uniform the ancient, Buddhist, and Mohammedan educational systems. Western education was open to all, regardless of caste or religion. In fact, some of the less privileged groups were the first to take advantage of it. Its emphasis on science and experiment brought a new element into Indian life. The establishment of universities as we find them today, encouraged the growth of a critical spirit and led to a questioning of old values. However, there was no attempt to combine the heritage of ancient, medieval and modern knowledge and develop a truly national system of education.[27]

When Mohammedan rulers were replaced by the British, the latter felt the need for doing something for the education of the people of India. So they started a British system of education. About it, the report of the University Education Commission comments thus:

> One of the noteworthy acts of Warren Hastings, the first Governor General, was to establish the Calcutta Madrasah which was intended "to qualify the sons of Mohammedan gentlemen for responsible and lucrative offices in the State" and the course of studies followed the traditional pattern embracing theology, logic, rhetoric, grammar, law, natural philosophy, astronomy, geometry and arithmetic . . . when the next important educational institution was established a few years later at Banaras, it was "for the preservation and cultivation of the Laws, Literature and Religion of the nation, to accomplish the same purpose of the Hindus as the Madrasah for the Mohammedans and specially to supply qualified Hindu assistants to European Judges".[28]

During the eighteenth and nineteenth centuries, the ancient, Buddhist and Mohammedan centres of learning were fast declining because of the unsettled political conditions in the country. It was at this time of Indian history that the British came to this country as traders and merchants and then they gradually increased their sphere of influence to become ultimately the masters of India. Here starts the modern period of Indian education.[29]

11

The origin of the system of modern education which is prevalent today can be traced to the beginning of the 19th century when the British rulers decided that the great objective of education ought to be the promotion of European literature and science among the natives of India; and that all the funds appropriated for the purpose of education would be best employed on English education alone. They also made provision to continue the schools and colleges where indigenous learning was imparted. The new schools that were opened by the British became popular because of great interest shown in English education by some of the educated Indians and leaders. "The education imparted in these schools became a guarantee for entry into Government service".[30]

There were many steps taken for the development of higher education in India during the British period. The Government of India appointed many commissions and committees between 1857 and 1947, such as the Indian Universities Commission (1902); Michael Sadler Commission (1919); Inter University Board of India and Ceylon (1924 to date); Hartog Committee (1929); and the University Grants Committee (1945-1947). One of the most important landmarks in university education was the Report of the Central Advisory Board of Education on Post-War Educational Development (1944), better known as the Sargent Report. It drew attention to the following defects in the Indian university system: (a) the undue importace attached to examinations; (b) the emphasis on book-learning as contrasted with original thinking; (c) the lack of personal contact between teachers and students; (d) the inadequacy of financial support from the state and from private benefactors, making it necessary for the universities to depend on examination fees, which leads to the deterioration of their standards; (e) the absence of schemes for assisting poor but able students; (f) the need for more universities.[31]

The Sargent scheme also suggested an all-India committee along the same lines as the University Grants Committee in Great Britain, consisting of a few eminent non-officials of university experience who would advise the central government as well as provincial governments on the allocation of grants from public funds and would also see that while each

12

university jealously guards its autonomy, it also
works for and not against the common good of all and
of the country as a whole. The work of this com-
ittee was to co-ordinate and unify the work of the
universities throughout India.[32]

FOOTNOTES

[1]Anathnath Basu, University, Education Past and Present in India (Calcutta: The Book Emporium, 1944), p. 1.

[2]S. M. Thingale and S. A. Paranjpe, Educational Problems and Administration in the Bombay State (Kolhapur: Arya Bhanu Press, 1956), pp. 349-350.

[3]William J. Haggerty, Higher and Professional Education in India, U.S. Department of Health, Education, and Welfare, Office of Education (Washington: U.S. Government Printing Office, 1969), p. 39.

[4]Ibid.

[5]S. R. Dongerkery, University Education in India (Bombay: P. S. Manaktala Sons Private Ltd., 1967), p. 1.

[6]India, The Report of the University Education Commission, 1948-49 (Delhi: The Government of India Press, 1950), pp. 7-8.

[7]Basu, op. cit., pp. 1-2.

[8]India, Ministry of Information and Broadcasting, Facts About India (New Delhi: The Government of India Printing Press, 1957), p. 143.

[9]T. N. Siqueira, The Education of India: History and Problems (4th ed., Bombay: Oxford University Press, 1952), p. 5.

[10]John Francis Cramer, George Stephenson Browne, and Willard B. Spalding, Contemporary Education (New York: Harcourt, Brace and World, 1956), pp. 513-514.

[11]Basu, op. cit., p. 6.

[12]National Council of Educational Research and Training, Second All-India Educational Survey (New Delhi: Indraprastha Press, 1967), p. 6.

[13]Basu, op. cit., pp. 8-9.

[14]Ibid., pp. 11-12.

[15]Second All-India Educational Survey, p. 6.

[16] *Report of the University Education Commission, 1948-1949,* p. 8.

[17] Dongerkery, *op. cit.,* pp. 8-9.

[18] Sequeira, *op. cit.,* p. 18.

[19] Humayun Kabir, *Education in New India* (New York: Harper and Brothers, 1955), pp. 107-108.

[20] Paul Monroe, *A Cyclopedia of Education* (New York: The Macmillan Company, 1918), III p. 400.

[21] Lewis Jennings Larson, "National Planning and Higher Education in India Since 1947" (Unpublished Ph.D. dissertation, Peabody College, 1964), pp. 39-40.

[22] Dongerkery, *op. cit.,* p. 15.

[23] Siqueira, *op. cit.,* p. 54.

[24] Haggerty, *op. cit.,* p. 42.

[25] Ministry of Information & Broadcasting, *Facts About India,* p. 143.

[26] Cramer, Browne and Spalding, *op. cit.,* p. 514.

[27] Kabir, *op. cit.,* p. 108.

[28] *The Report of the University Education Commission, 1948-49,* pp. 8-9.

[29] Basu, *op. cit.,* p. 12.

[30] *Second All India Education Survey,* p. 6.

[31] Dongerkery, *op. cit.,* pp. 46-47.

[32] Siqueira, *op. cit.,* pp. 238-239.

15

CHAPTER II

THE ROLE OF HIGHER EDUCATION

This chapter is concerned with the role of higher education in India since Independence (1947). The general aims and functions, legal status, the State's role and the Federal or Central Government role and function with regard to higher education will be considered here. Great changes have taken place in the political and economic condition of India since August 15, 1947. Considerable changes and progress have also taken place in the field of higher education. The Report of the University Education Commission of 1948-1949 describes the changes and progress in these words:

> We have now a wider conception
> of the duties and responsibilities
> of universities. They have to
> provide leadership in politics
> and administration, the professions,
> industry and commerce. They have
> to meet the increasing demand
> for every type of higher education,
> literary and scientific, technical
> and professional. They must enable
> the country to attain, in as short
> a time as possible, freedom from
> want, disease and ignorance, by
> the application and development
> of scientific and technical knowl-
> edge. India is rich in natural
> resources and her people have
> intelligence and energy and are
> throbbing with renewed life and
> vigour. It is for the universities
> to create knowledge and train
> minds who would bring together
> the two, material resources and
> human energies. If our living
> standards are to raised, a radical
> change of spirit is essential.[1]

17

The General Aims and Functions of Higher Education

The late Prime Minister of India, Jawaharlal Nehru, once spoke of the aims and functions of university education thus: "A University stands for humanism, for tolerance, for reason, for progress, for the adventure of ideas, and for the research of truth. It stands for the onward march of the human race towards even higher objectives. If the universities discharge their duties adequately, then it is well with the nations and the people."[2]

The major functions of higher education include more than mere preparation of specialized jobs. A university has no place for communal elements or sectionalism. It must be for the welfare of the nation and the people. In this context Mahadma Gandhi's concept of education and its aims are noteworthy. His education was designed to produce moral and spiritual men and women. For Gandhiji, religion and education were complimentary to each other. Education had to take into account the development of an individual's moral and spiritual powers. Modern education on the other hand, ignored soul and therefore all the powers and possibilities of soul were held in abeyance for the more material aims to be achieved. Materialism as aginst spiritualism was being emphasized.[3]

It implies that true education is not mere perusal of prescribed courses of studies. It is the harmonious development of the mental, physical, social and spiritual powers. A Christian writer's concept of the aim of education is quite similar to that of Gandiji:

> Our ideas of education take too
> narrow and too low a range. There
> is need of a broader scope, a
> higher aim. True education means
> more than the pursual of a certain
> course of study. It means more
> than a preparation for the life
> that now is. It has to do with
> the whole being, and with the
> whole period of existence possible
> to man. It is the harmonious
> development of the physical, the

mental, and the spiritual powers.
It prepares the student for the
joy of service in this world,
and for the higher joy of wider
service in the world to come.[4]

Chaliha also emphasized the importance of
building up the total man. "Our duties as teachers
should not be confined to the classroom but to every
aspect of the student's day-to-day activities. It
is in this context that we talk of the ideal teacher,
who becomes the real friend, philosopher and guide
to the students around."[5]

Shrisuraj Bhan points out Tagore's view point:
The most important factor in education must be the
inspiring atmosphere of creative activity. Therefore
the primary function of our university, he says, should
be the constructive work of knowledge. People should
be brought together for their intellectual exploration
and creation; and the teaching should be like the
overflow of water of this spring of culture, spon-
taneous and inevitable. "Education can only become
natural and wholesome when it is the direct fruit
of living and growing knowledge."[6] Another great
educator of India, Shri Jatadhari Misra, expressed
this point of view: "The aim of education is to build
a perfect man, a fully responsible, controlled and
disciplined future citizen of the country. Education
is not partial."[7]

Dr. Zakir Hussain, late President of the Indian
Republic, during his visit to Hungary, had the degree
of Doctor of Laws conferred upon him by the University of Budapest. During the course of his speech
there, he is reported to have said:

The role of education in such
a rapidly changing world based
on an evergrowing explosing of
knowledge has to be far different
from what it was in the past.
In the traditional societies,
the emphasis in education was
on the 'preservation' of knowledge.
It has now to be shifted to research or 'acquisition' of new
knowledge.[8]

19

Prime Minister Indira Ghandi commented that
education is not just the passing of examinations
or gathering of knowledge. "It is training of the
mind," she said, "to think and to judge; to discriminate between what is of true value and the ex-
citement of a passing fad; to tolerate sincere differences of opinion or customs, but to be intolerant
of insincerity, hypocrisy and shoddiness no less than
of crime and evil"[9]

In her inaugural address at the Vice-Chancellors'
Conference held in September 1967 in New Delhi,
Shrimati Indira Gandhi further pointed out the role of
higher education:

> Education is, of course, one of
> the vital elements in the life
> of any nation and it must respond
> to the changing needs of the nation.
> In our country, we have all these
> problems which the other countries
> face and we have also a lot of
> extra problems. We have had vast
> quantitative increase in education.
> The demand for education is a
> growing one and it is insatiable.
> This very democratization of educa-
> tion raises problems for us.
> Education must serve the needs
> of change, growth and moderni-
> zation. At the same time it must
> strengthen our unity. It should
> inculcate in our young men and
> women an outlook of tolerance and
> rationality. While we cannot
> avoid increasing quantity, we
> must at the same time try to encour-
> age quality and foster excellence.[10]

P.N. Kirpal, Secretary, Ministry of Education,
in his welcome address at the fifth conference of
Vice-Chancellors of Indian universities, convened
jointly by the Ministry of Education and the University Grants Commission held in September, 1967,
emphasized the aims and importance of the universities:

The strength of any educational
system, the contribution it can
make to national integration,
national development and the re-
surgence of modern and social
values, is always reflected in
the vitality and functioning of
the universities. The universities
create the intelligentsia which
must play a dominant role in bind-
ing the nation together in the
pursuit of common fundamental
goals. The project of the universities determine the efficiency
of the school system and the nature
and success of all difficult
school programmes of education.
It is primarily on the university
that the society depends for the
formulation, development and
spread of human values, which
determine the morale and character
of the individual and the quality
of the culture of the society.[11]

Humayun Kabir urged the leaders to offer equal
opportunities to all, by providing equal facilities
and educational opportunities for all its citizen.
He also pointed out the necessity of the universal
aspect of education.[12]

The future of any country depends mainly on its
educational programme, especially upon the institutions of higher education for its leadership. Wood
emphasized its importance explicitly.[13] Dongerkery
supported Woods' point of view of stating that one
of the most important functions of universities is
to provide leadership in the professions and in other
walks of life.[14] He commented about the two main
functions of universities and stated that "Teaching
or the dessemination of knowledge, and research, or
the advancement of knowledge, have been accepted as
the two main functions of a modern university."[15]

The university has a social responsibility to
perform. It should serve as the intellectual conscience of the community. It should be a national

21

bulwark against all that is false, trivial, showy and unworthy. It must be the place where ideas and values are criticized and evaluated; and where false doctrines and nonsense are exposed for what they are. It should be noted, however, that universities can discharge this function only in a free society. Another social responsibility of the university is to promote human relations.[16]

A.N. Jha, Secretary, Ministry of Information and Broadcasting, stated that the real problems of education today are to be centred on the need to develop people capable of living the fullest possible lives. We shall have to produce men and women who are able to understand the significance of the past, who are in the stream of current ideas and who can make use of them and who have the quality of imagination that is capable of foreseeing and welcoming the future. After pointing out the difficulties of devising an educational system which would achieve all these ends, he suggested certain lines of thought which might be usefully pursued. He continues:

> In the days to come, I suggest
> we shall find it impossible to
> consider anybody as adequately
> educated if he or she does not
> understand at least some science.
> Neither shall we be able to regard
> as an educated man, a technician
> or a scientist, however distinguished,
> who had failed to develop a sub-
> stantial interest in the humanities
> and the arts, or who shows no
> evidence of being aware of the
> significance of society and his
> part in it.[17]

At the meeting of the Council of Association of Commonwealth Universities held in India on January 13, 1970, inaugurated by Professor V.K.R.V. Rao, the former Union Minister for Education and Youth, emphasis was laid on the role of education. Underlining the role of universities in developing countries, Dr. Rao said that two eminent functions of the university—pursuit of truth and excellence and training for leading —continue to retain their significance. He emphasized the university's responsibility of cultivation of

a sense of social responsibility, adult education
and identification and involvement by way of service
to the local communities. Dr. Rao also suggested
that it was essential to allow students to participate[18]
in the management of university affairs.

Gangulee, former Counsellor (Education and Culture), Embassy of India, wrote an article in "India
News," in which he stated that the main aim of higher
education during the course of the next five years
would be:

> Expansion and improvement of science
> education and teachers' training;
> improvement of standards of post-
> graduate education and research;
> development of Indian languages
> and book production, especially
> textbooks; and the consolidation
> of technical education and its
> closer linking with the needs
> of industry and its orientation
> towards self-employment. Emphasis
> will also be laid on the development
> of youth services. Greater use
> will be made of educational tech-
> nologies, such as part-time and
> correspondence courses, modern
> media of communication, which
> promote expansion and development
> with minimum investment and without[19]
> lowering standards.

Many steps have been taken to reorganize secondary
and higher education and promote rapid expansion of
scientific and technical education necessary for development of industry and agriculture; to fulfill the
democratic ideal of providing equality of opportunity
to all members of the community; and to bring about
rapid changes in the political, social and economic[20]
life of the country.

In his book, "Some Aspects of University Education," Jha emphasized the role or function of university
education:

The educational authorities, with
the full support of the Government,
should institute a course of training
which would be specifically aimed
at creating a new breed of administrators,
leaders in Government and managers
of Industry. The type of person
I have in mind must not be a scientist
or a technologist alone. Indeed
this would be dangerous. It is
essential that the Government
of the nation and the management
of its institutions should be
in the hands of broadly educated
people trained to appreciate and
evaluate developments.[21]

One of the aims of higher education is to provide
a society with good and competent men and women, well
trained administrators, leaders in Government, managers
of industry, arts, technology, medicine, agriculture
and other areas. The higher education in India is
gradually becoming an effective instrument in the
political, social and economic transformation of the
country. Expenditure on education is most productive
investment that a country can make for developing
social, economic, and political growth. The universities and colleges in India are engaged in a most chal-
lenging and rewarding task.[22]

The basic role of higher education in India should
be, urged the Education Commission, to promote a sense
of common citizenship and perpetuate its culture,
to further national integration, to make a direct
contribution to national productivity, and to contribute
to the world stock of rapidly expanding knowledge
and technology.

If education is to play its role in raising national productivity, the educational system must be
closely related to national needs of trained manpower
in industry and agriculture, of trade and commerce
and administration and management. Regarding it,
Dr. Kothari, former Chairman of the University Grants
Commission, said: "Education is a major factor in
the industrialization of agriculture. Again we need
to encourage research of the highest institutions,

and in this connection it has to be recognized that research is of no value unless it is of first-rate quality. The second best will not do."[23]

The Report of the University Education Commission summarized the aims of education as follows:

> Democracy depends for its very life on a high standard of general, vocational and professional education. Dissemination of learning, incessant search for new knowledge, unceasing effort to plumb the meaning of life, provision for professional education to satisfy the occupational needs of our society are the vital tasks of higher education. There must be a sufficient unity of purpose in all this diversity to produce a community of values and ideas among educated men. Our policies and programmes must be brought into line with the social purposes which we profess to serve. We may use various institutional forms as time and circumstances may require but we must be steadfastly loyal to the abiding elements of respect for human personality, freedom of belief and expression for all citizens, a deep obligation to promote human well-being, faith in reason and humanity.[24]

The Commission, after enumerating the factors which contribute to the greatness of a country, points out the characteristics of one who claims to be civilized:

> If we claim to be civilized, we must develop thought for the poor and the suffering, chivalrous regard and respect for women, faith in human brotherhood regardless of race or color, nation or religion, love of peace and freedom, abhorrence of cruelty

25

and ceaseless devotion to the
claims of justice.[25]

Broadly, the functions of the universities in
the modern world may be said to be the following:
(1) To seek and cultivate new knowledge, to engage
vigorously and fearlessly in the pursuit of truth,
and to interpret old knowledge, and benefits in the
light of new needs and discoveries. (2) To provide
the right kind of leadership in all walks of life,
to identify gifted youth and help them develop their
potential to the fullness by cultivation of physical
fitness, developing the powers of the mind and culti-
vating right interests, attitudes and moral and intellectual values. (3) To provide society with competent
men and women trained in agriculture, arts, medicine,
science and technology and various other professions,
who will also be cultivated individuals, imbued with
a sense of social purpose. (4) Strive to promote
equality and social justice and to reduce social and
cultural differences through diffusion of education.
(5) To foster in the teachers and students, and through
them in society generally, the attitudes and values
needed for developing the good life in individual
and society. (6) To provide part-time and correspondence courses and extension programmes of various
kinds so as to provide varied educational facilities
for widening clientele. (7) To undertake carefully
worked out programmes for school improvement.[26]

To sum up, the general aims of university education
are: (a) teaching, (b) service, (c) research, (d)
personality building, and (e) learning.

The Legal Status of Higher Education

The Constitution of India provides equal opportunity to everyone regardless of color, creed, race,
caste or language, according to his potentials. Such
democratic principles are embodied in the Constitution:

> WE, THE PEOPLE OF INDIA, having
> solemnly resolved to constitute
> India into a SOVEREIGN DEMOCRATIC
> REPUBLIC and to secure all its
> citizens: JUSTICE, social, economic
> and political; LIBERTY of thought,

26

expression, belief, faith and
worship; EQUALITY of status and
of opportunity; and to promote
among them all FRATERNITY assuring
the dignity of the individual
and the unity of the Nation; IN
OUR CONSTITUENT ASSEMBLY DO HEREBY
ADOPT, ENACT AND GIVE TO OURSELVES
THIS CONSTITUTION.[27]

The fundamental rights are classified as:

1. Right to Equality,
2. Right to Freedom,
3. Right against Exploitation,
4. Right to Freedom of Religion,
5. Cultural and Education Rights,
6. Right to Property and
7. Right to Constitutional Remedies.[28]

Every citizen has the right of education according
to the Constitution of India:

All minorities, religious or linguistic, have been given the right
to establish and administer educational institutions and the State
is prohibited from discrimination
against any such institution in
granting aid. Further, no citizen
can be denied admission to educational institutions maintained
or aided by the state on grounds
only of religion, race, caste
or language. Thus, in addition
to their own, the minorities in
India have all the educational
facilities available to the majority.[29]

State Role in Higher Education

According to the provisions laid down in the
Constitution, education is essentially a service which
comes under state jurisdiction. All important policy
decisions concerning education are taken by the state
governments, even in higher education. Universities
are established through the enactments passed by the

state legislatures, and the colleges are set up with their approval.

There are twenty-two states and nine Union territories in India at present. (See Appendix C.) The organizational structure of the system of education varies from state to state. The basic structure, however, has undergone little change over the last 35 years. Regarding the organizational structure of the educational system, the Ministry of Education states:

> In every state there is an Education
> Minister at the apex assisted
> by an Education Secretary. In
> some states there is also a Deputy
> Minister of Education. The Depart-
> ment of Education has two main
> organs: (1) the secretariat,
> which has a policy making and
> coordination function, and (2)
> the directorate of education which
> performs the functions of direction,
> regulation and inspection.
>
> The directorate of education which
> is the "hard core" of the machinery
> of educational administration
> in each state has developed a
> tendency in recent years to be
> concerned mainly with the school
> level of education. The establishment
> of independent directorates of
> collegiate and technical education
> is another recent trend noticeable
> in some states. In some states,
> technical education is administered
> by the Department of Industry,
> in others, by the Public Works
> Department.[30]

The new Constitution of India provides for the continuation of state pre-eminence in educational jurisdiction. With regard to the opening of new universities, the University Education Commission has recommended that "before any new university is established, it would be desirable for the State Governments concerned to prepare, in consultation with the University Grants

Commission, a prospective plan for the next 5 to 10 years taking into account the available resources and facilities and the need for further development and expansion of higher education."[31]

All the universities (except the centrally administered universities) have been created by state legislatures. Though they are dependent on the central or state governments, as the case may be, for their constitution and powers, all the universities enjoy the measure of autonomy in their internal administration.[32]

D.M. Desai, the former Prime Minister and Finance Minister of India, emphasized the absolute power of state governments in education: "The Constitution of India vests the state governments with almost absolute authority in education including university education, leaving to the Federal Government (Central) only a limited role of offering advice, providing leadership."[33]

Central or Federal Government Role in Higher Education

Though the apparent constitutional position is that states play the chief role in determining the nature, size, and pace of development of higher education in their own territories, the actual position is otherwise. Since the attainment of independence, the Central Government has shown a more pervasive and a more active interest in the development of university education and all other levels as well. Desai states three events of great significance which have relegated the states to a subordinate position, giving a dominant and decisive position to the centre:

> One relates to the fact that substantial grants are now being made available to the States by the Centre to be undertaken on large scales, a variety of programmes for the internal transformation and enrichment of different fields and types of institutions. The second major event is the launching of a programme of reconstruction and development of education through

29

the Five-Year Plans. This has
shifted the focus of authority
to the Centre, as it fixes the
priorities and allocates funds
for planned development. The
third great event has been the
establishment of University Grants
Commission which has been, since
1953, the main agency of the union
Government to coordinate developments in higher education, determine
standards and disburse grants
to all universities. The institution of the University Grants
Commission and its increasing
developments has again considerably
limited the absolute authority
vested in State Governments in
respect of higher education.[34]

The 1969 Reference Annual of India also describes
the role of the Central of Federal Government: Education
is primarily the responsibility of state governments,
the Federal Government concerning itself with the
co-ordination of the educational facilities and determination of standards in respect of higher education
(through the University Grants Commission) and research
and scientific and technical education. Co-ordination
in regard to other sectors of education is secured
through a standing committee of the Central Advisory
Board of Education. The Federal Government is also
responsible for the running of five universities (Aligarh, Banaras, Delhi, Visva Bharati and Jawaharlal
Nehru) and such other institutions of national importance as parliament may by law declare.

The Central Advisory Board of Education lays
down the general education policy. Its four standing
committees dealing with elementary, secondary, university and social education, formulate aims and objectives, assess prevailing positions and draw up future
plans in their respective fields. A steering committee
of the Board co-ordinate their activities.[35]

Though, as noted above, the new Constitution
of India has vested absolute responsibility of education
upon the state governments, it has, by Article 246,

30

given to the Central Government the function of co-
ordination and determination of standards in institutions for higher education or research including scientific and technical institutions.[36] "A working partnership has been evolved between the Union and the
State Governments for implementing educational development plans."[37]

One of the important roles of higher education
is to strengthen national unity. This goal cannot
be reached until India has a national system of education. Realizing this problem, Kabir stated: "The
absence of a common system of national education has
been one of the main reasons why so many Indians ex-
hibit even today a regional, linguistic or communal
outlook."[38]

In order to strengthen national unity and national
system of education, the Government of India has adapted
a national policy on education, based on the 1966
Commission Report:

> Education is powerful instrument
> of national development—social,
> economic and cultural. The highest
> priority should, therefore, be
> accorded to the development of
> a national system of education
> which will accelerate the transfor-
> mation of the existing system
> into a new one based on principles
> of justice, equality, liberty
> and dignity of the individual,
> enshrined in the Constitution
> of India; provide adequate and
> equal opportunity to every child
> and help him to develop his person-
> ality to its fullest; make the
> rising generation conscious of
> the fundamental unity of the country
> in the midst of her great future
> and emphasize science and technology
> and the cultivation of moral,
> social and spiritual values.
> This policy statement goes on:
> The most important and urgent
> reform needed is to transform

the existing system of education
in order to strengthen national
unity, promote social integration,
accelerate economic growth and
general moral, social and spiritual
values.³⁹

University Autonomy

Indian universities do not have as much autonomy
as the universities of the United States and Great
Britain. All the universities in India are under
the control of the state government, except the five
Central Government universities (Aligarh, Banaras,
Delhi, Visva Bharati and Jawaharlal Nehru University).
Soon after Independence, several attempts have been
made to change this government dominion. The <u>Report
of the University Education Commission</u> elaborates
on this point:

> Freedom of individual development
> is the basis of democracy. Exclusive
> control of education by the state
> has been an important factor in
> facilitating the maintenance of
> totalitarian tyrannies. In such
> state institutions of higher learning
> controlled and managed by govern-
> mental agencies act like mercenaries,
> promote the political purposes
> of the state, make them acceptable
> to an increasing number of their
> population and supply them with
> the weapons they need. We must
> resist, in the interest of our
> own democracy, the trend towards
> the governmental domination of
> the educational process.
>
> Higher education is, undoubtedly,
> an obligation of the state but
> state aid is not to be confused
> with state control over academic
> policies and practices. Intellectual
> progress demands the maintenance
> of the spirit of free enquiry.
> The pursuit and practice of truth

regardless of consequences
has the ambition of universities.
Their prayer is that of the dying
Goethe: "More light" or that
of Ajax in the mist "Light, though
I perish in the light."

Professional integrity requires
that teachers should be as free
to speak on controversial issues
as any other citizens of a free
country. An atmosphere of freedom
is essential for developing this
"morality of the mind."[40]

The above report makes it clear that in a free
and democratic state, education should be free from
state or governmental control and that the control
of edication by state is a feature of totalitarian
tyrannies.

All of the 50-odd witnesses examined by the Rad-
hakrishan Committee on this subject expressed themselves emphatically in favor of maintaining autonomy
of the universities. Earlier in 1932, the same view
had been expressed by those who appeared before the
Sadler Commission on education. Even this Commission
itself upheld the principle of autonomy.

Varma, recognizing the importance of university
autonomy, pointed out that a university cannot be
in a position to discharge its functions effectively
without an appreciable measure of autonomy. Its main
functions, he states, should be teaching, research
and service to the community. Only an autonomous
institution, free from regimentation of ideas and
pressure of party or power politics, can pursue truth
fearlessly and build up, in its teachers and students,
habits of independent thinking and a spirit of enquiry
unfettered by the limitations and prejudices of the
near and the immediate, which is so essential for
the development of a free society.[41]

University autonomy, on the other hand, has its
sphere mainly in the following: (a) the selection
of students; (b) the determination of courses of study
and methods of teaching; and (d) the selection of

areas and problems of research. In using its autonomy, a university must be governed by one overriding consideration of its commitment to truth in all fields of activity.[42]

Varma viewed university autonomy to be functioning at three overlapping levels: (1) autonomy within a university; (2) autonomy of a university in relation to the university system as a whole (the autonomy of one university in relation to another or in relation to the University Grants Commission and the Inter Community Board); and (3) autonomy of the university system as a whole, including the UGC and the IUB and in relation to agencies and influences emanating outside the university system, the most important of which are the central and the state governments.[43]

The proper sphere of university autonomy lies in the selection of students, the appointment and promotion of teachers and the determination of courses of study, methods of teaching, the selection of areas and problems of research.

Autonomy within the universities:

1. The universities should give considerable autonomy to its departments. Wider administrative and financial powers should be delegated to a Committee of Management to be set up in each department under the chairmanship of the head of the department.

2. The freedom and autonomy of colleges must be recognized and respected in the same spirit as the university wants for itself.

3. There should be joint committee of teachers and students in each department and in every college, and a central committee under the chairmanship of the head of the institution for the discussion of common problems and difficulties. Student representation should also be associated with the academic councils and the courts of universities.

4. A suitable machinery for consultations
   between universities, the UGC, the
   Inter-University Board and the Government should be developed for reaching
   decision regarding number of students
   to be trained, courses of study and
   problems of applied research.[44]

It is therefore, very important to safeguard
the universities against any kind of encroachment
on its activities. The state control may be minimal,
limited to the requirements of proper utilization
of funds and conformity to the broad objectives of
national policy. "Beyond this, any attempt on the
part of politicians to interfere in the university
affairs is bound to be harmful."[45]

Though Indian universities are controlled by
the states, they enjoy autonomy in their internal
administration. As Dongerkery points out, "The Indian
Universities today enjoy the greatest measure of autonomy in their internal administration. In this respect,
they may be described as standing midway between the
British universities, on one side, and the continental
universities, on the other."[46]

35

FOOTNOTES

[1] _The Report of the University Education Commission, 1948-49_, p. 33.

[2] _Humanism and Education: Nehru's Speeches_ Vol 1, p. 335, Quoted in Ranjendra pal Singh, _Nehru on Education_ (Jullunder, Delhi 6: Sterling Publishers Ltd., 1966), p. 3.

[3] _Ibid._, p. 42.

[4] Ellen G. White, _Education_ (Mountain View, California: Pacific Press Publishing Association, 1903), p. 13. -

[5] Shri Parag Chaliha, "Some Thoughts on College Education," _Development of Education in New India_, ed. by N. B. Sen (New Book Society of India), p. 84.

[6] Shrisuraj Bhan, "A Decennium of Higher Education" in _Development of Education in New India_, ed. by N. B. Sen (New Delhi: New Book Society of India, 1966), p. 16.

[7] _Ibid._, p. 37.

[8] _Educational India_, XXXV (August, 1968), 66.

[9] _Weekly India News_, Embassy of India, IV (February 4, 1966), 5.

[10] India, University Grants Commission, _Vice-Chancellors' Conference_ (New Delhi: September, 1967), p. 3.

[11] _Ibid._, p. 1.

[12] Kabir, _op. cit._, pp. 104-105.

[13] Hugh E. Wood, "Higher Education in India," _Teachers College Record_, IV (May, 1954), 418.

[14] Dongerkery, _op. cit._, p. 211.

[15] _Ibid._, p. 135.

[16] K. Satchidananda Murty, "University and Good Citizenship," _The Educational Quarterly_, (June, 1959), 157-158.

[17] A. N. Jha, "Some Aspects of University Education," _Indian Education: Journal of the All-India Federation of Educational Association_ (December 1965-January 1966), 181.

[18]"Chronicle of Higher Education and Research in India,"
University News, VIII (February, 1970), 3.

[19]Gangulee, "Education in India Since Independence: Progress
and Problem," India News, VIII (February 20, 1970), 3.

[20]Weekly India News, VII (July 5, 1968), 4.

[21]Jha, op. cit., p. 19.

[22]Education in Eighteen Years of Freedom, pp. 37-38.

[23]University Grants Commission, Vice-Chancellors' Conference,
September, 1967, p. 24.

[24]The Report of the University Education Commission, 1948-
1949, p. 66.

[25]Ibid.

[26]J. C. Aggarwal, Major Recommendations of the Education
Commission, 1964-66 (New Delhi: Arya Book Depot, 1966), p. 122.

[27]India's Constitution, Publications Division (New Delhi:
Ministry of Information and Broadcasting, Government of India,
1969), p. 10.

[28]Ibid., p. 21.

[29]Ibid., p. 26.

[30]Education in Eighteen Years of Freedom, pp. 11-12.

[31]University Grants Commission, Handbook of Universities
of India (New Delhi: Government Printing Press, 1964), pp. 2-3.

[32]University Grants Commission, Hand Book of Universities
of India (New Delhi: Government Printing Press, 1964), pp. 2-3.

[33]D. M. Desai, "Government and Private Agencies in the
Administration of Higher Education," Education Quarterly, (October,
1967), 17.

[34]Ibid.

[35]Ministry of Information and Broadcasting, India, A Reference Annual (Fairidabad: Government of India Press, 1969), p. 60.

[36]Report of the University Grants Commission, December 1953-March 1957, pp. 2-3.

[37]Weekly India News, V (July, 1966), 5.

[38]Kabir, op. cit., p. 110.

[39]India News, VIII (February, 1970), 3.

[40]The Report of the University Education Commission, 1948-49, pp. 48-49.

[41]D. C. Varma, "University Autonomy," The Education Quarterly, (October, 1967), 8.

[42]Ibid.

[43]Ibid., pp. 8-9.

[44]Kothari Commission Recommendations and Evaluations, pp. 115-116.

[45]Varma, op. cit., p. 10.

[46]Dongerkery, op. cit., p. 77.

CHAPTER III

ORGANIZATION AND ADMINISTRATION OF HIGHER EDUCATION

The modern institution of higher learning in India
got its start in 1857, when the British Government char-
tered the first three universities. Located in Delhi,
Bombay, and Calcutta, these schools were patterned after
the British Universities. After ninety years of direct
British rule, India had only 19 universities and 422
colleges to serve a population of about 350 million. In
1982, after 35 years of independence, India had increased the number of universities to 137, seven times
the total at the date of independence, and the colleges to
to 4,558 serving a population of about 700 million. The
total enrollment of students in these universities and
colleges has increased by 2.6 million.[1] The progress of
university education is geographically presented in
Appendix A. This tremendous growth in the number of
colleges and universities, along with the upswing in
student enrollment naturally increased the difficulty
of the administrative and organizational task. It is
the purpose of this chapter to point out some of the
special aspects of internal and external organizational
structure of higher educational institutions and their
administration.

External Organization and administration

The external organizational authorities who administer and control the institutions of higher education
in India are: (1) the central or Union Government
(Federal) acting through the Ministry of Education
(2) the State Government working through its Ministry
of Education and the Education Department (3) the philanthropic and religious organizations (Voluntary
Organization).

The Central or Union Government

The educational responsibilities of the Government
of India are mainly discharged by the Ministry of Education. There are two Ministries, namely the Ministry
of Education and the Ministry of Scientific Research
and Cultural Affairs. India gives numerous responsibilities to the Union Ministry of Education. The Ministry
of Education describes its organizational structure
in this way:

39

As organized at present, the
Ministry of Education consists
of nine Divisions, one each for
Administrative, Elementary and
Basic Education Scholarships,
Research and Publications, and
Social Welfare. The Ministry
also has, jointly with the Min-
istry of Scientific Research and
Cultural Affairs, a cadre of
advisory officers which at present
consists of six Deputy Educational
Advisers, twenty-five Assistant
Educational Advisers, twenty Ed-
ucational Officers and seven
Assistant Education Officers.[2]

The Central Government functions as a clearing
house for educational information. The idea of the
clearing house function was first put forward by the
Indian Education Commission (1882). This tradition
has not only been continued but also greatly expanded
since independence. The Government of India supplies
three annual publications: (1) Education in India (in
two volumes); (2) Education in the States; and (3) Education in Indian Universities. Besides, it also publishes a Directory of Institutions of Higher Education
which first began as an annual publication, but has
now been made biennial. The publication of periodical
statistical data or progress reports is only a part
of the clearing house function of the Central Government.
This function also includes the surveys and publications
of studies, reports of commissions and committees and
such other educational documents as are necessary for
broadcasting significant educational ideas and development.[3]

Probably the oldest function of the government
of India is to administer education in the Union
Territories or Centrally Administered Areas. This function dates back to 1870 when educational authority was
decentralized and transferred to the provinces. But
the Central Government retained authority for areas
which were too small to be given the status of a province, such as Coorg.

In 1947, the centrally administered areas were
only five: Delhi, Ajmer, Mervar, Nicobar, and Andaman
Islands, Coorg and Panth Piploda. By the end of

1947, the number of Centrally Administered Areas had increased. Thus, at present there are six Union Territories, administered directly by the Central Government of India.[4]

The Ministry of Education has set up a number of advisory bodies which function in different sectors of education. The oldest and the most important of these is the Central Advisory Board of Education. The Board is chaired by the Union Minister of Education and membership includes all Educational Ministers of States. Until 1947, it was the only body which considered the national problems of education and gave necessary advice to the Central and State Government.[5]

Due to the increased volume of educational activity, in the post-independence period, it was felt desirable to constitute a number of other advisory bodies to deal with special sectors of education. At present, there are 15 such bodies which bring official and nonofficial workers together for consideration of educational problems and to render advice to the Central and State Government on issues which are of importance in formulating educational policies and programmes. They also bring to bear an all-India approach to the problems entrusted to them. A practice of holding periodical conferences of State Education Ministers to discuss important educational matters is also growing.[6]

The Government of India also undertakes the collection and dissemination of educational information for the country as a whole. It strives to provide stimulating national leadership in education development and financial assistance to State Government for their educational programmes.[7]

Attached to the Central Advisory Board of Education (CABE) is the Central Bureau of Education. It works through two sections which respectively deal with overseas and internal information. It indexes and analyses the information collected and publishes annual reports. It also maintains an excellent library. Another important organ of the Ministry is the Overseas Information Bureau, which supplies the most recent information to Students' Advisory Bureaus of different States and universities. It also publishes a monthly bulletin, furnishing the latest information regarding educational facilities available abroad.[8]

41

Besides these agencies, the Central Government is helped and advised by a number of bodies constituted for different branches of education: University Grants Commission, (UGC) All-India Council for Secondary Education (AICSE), All-India Council of Elementary Education (AICEE), National Council for Women's Education and the National Council for Rural Higher Education.[9]

The Ministry of Scientific Research and Cultural Affairs was established in 1958. It is under the charge of a Minister of State. The Ministry is responsible for: (1) Cultural activities, (2) Scientific Research and Survey, and (3) Technical and Scientific education. It also exercises administrative control over 21 national laboratories and institutes, the Geodetic Survey of India, the Zoological Survey of India, the Botanical Survey of India, and the Central Board of Geophysics. The Ministry also conducts a number of institutions: the Indian School of Mines and Applied Geology, Dhanbad; Delhi Polytechnic; the Indian Institute of Technology, Kharagpur; the Indian National Scientific Documentation Centre, New Delhi, etc. Apart from these, it exercises limited control over a number of scientific organizations and institutions by giving them liberal grants-in-aid for the promotion of scientific and technical research.[10]

The Constitution of India defines, more clearly than that of the United States, the Educational responsibility of both the Federal and State Governments. "Because of the political and economic power of the Federal Government and the extent to which education is becoming a matter of national interest, the Federal Government in India will probably increase its influence in educational development, particularly in the field of higher education.[11]

Recent developments in the field of higher education such as the University Education Commissions, the University Grants Commissions, the Five-Year Plans indicate that the Central Government is gaining more control over educational enterprises.

Naik cites three developments which have partly reduced the States' educational responsibility. They are: (1) the desire, partly initiated by Gandhi, to develop "a national system of education for the country as a whole;" (2) the revival of appropriations in the form of grants to the states by the Federal Government to help finance public education; and (3) "the adoption of centralized planning and the creation of the Planning Commission" at the national level.[12]

Like the United States, the Indian Federal Government functions as a clearing house for giving educational information. In the United States, the main functions of the Federal Government are advisory in nature, though it also provides substantial amounts of money to the universities as grants-in-aids. The Federal Government of India is also advisory, but it provides more money to the universities and colleges than does the United States. The money is provided through the University Grants Commission, as in the British Government. Even the salaries of the teaching staff are sent through the University Grants Commission. The Indian Federal Government thus has a great deal of power and control over the institutions of higher learning.

Is such central control necessary? Cormack says: "Although theoretically decentralized India gives enormous responsibility to the Union Ministry of Education, and until States are better able to exercise their own leadership, this central coordination and guidance will be necessary.[13] If this assumption has any weight, then it is time that full responsibility be given to those States which have proved their ability to exercise their own leadership.

University Education Commission (1948-49) Report

The first action of real importance to be taken by the Government of India, soon after the Independence in the field of education, was the appointment of a University Education Commission, in 1948, under the chairmanship of Dr. Radhakrishanan, former President of India, eminent scholar, and former Vice-Chancellor of Benaras University. Associated with him were nine other men of distinction in the university world, including two Americans and one Briton.[14]

> The Commission appointed by the Government of India on 4 November 1948 'to report on Indian University Education and suggest improvements and extensions that may be desirable to suit present and future requirements of the

country,' is likely to go down
in history as a landmark in the
long course of higher education
in this country. Consisting of
ten members, including S. James
Duff of Durham and Drs. Arthur
Morgan and John Tigert from the
United States, with Dr. S. Radhakrishnan as Chairman, it toured
the whole of India visiting all
the university centres, inter-
viewing teachers, students, Ministers, Vice-Chancellors and Syn-
dics. It published the first
volume of its Report in 1949,
in 747 formidable pages setting
out a wealth of observation and
wisdom which though it bears the
marks of diverse hands will make
a fairly good textbook for teachers and educationists for many
years.[15]

"The report of the Commission is a comprehensive
document and it has far-reaching influence on the reconstruction of university education in recent years."[16]
The terms of reference of the commission were to consider
and make recommendation in regard to:

1. The aims and objectives of university education and research in India.

2. The changes considered necessary and desirable
   in the constitution's control, the functions
   and jurisdiction of universities in India
   and their relations with Governments, Central
   and Provincial.

3. The Finance of universities.

4. The maintenance of the highest standards of
   teaching and examination in the universities
   and colleges under their control.

5. The courses of study in the universities with
   special reference to the maintenance of a
   sound balance between the Humanities and the
   Sciences and between pure science and techno-

44

logical training and the duration of such
courses.

6. The standards of admission to university courses
of study with reference to the desirability
of an independent university entrance examination and the avoidance of unfair discriminations
which militate against Fundamental Right 23 (2).

7. The medium of instruction in the universities.

8. The provision for advanced study in Indian
culture, history, literature, languages,
philosophy and fine arts.

9. The need for more universities on a regional
or other basis.

10. The organization of advanced research in all
branches of knowledge in the universities
and institutes of higher research in a well
co-ordinated fashion avoiding waste of effort
and resources.

11. Religious instruction in the universities.

12. The special problems of the Banaras Hindu
University, the Aligarh Muslim University,
the Delhi University and other institutions
of an all-India character.

13. The qualifications, conditions of service,
salaries, privileges and functions of teachers
and the encouragement of original research
by teachers.

14. The discipline of students, hostels and the
organization of tutorial work and any other
matter which is germane and essential to a
complete and comprehensive enquiry into all
aspects of university education and advanced
research in India.[17]

Finally the Educational Commission Recommended:

1. that the standard of admission to university
courses should correspond to that of the present intermediate examination, i.e., after
the completion of 12 years of study at a school
and an intermediate college;

45

2. that in each province a large number of well-
    equipped and well-staffed intermediate colleges
    (with classes IX to XII or VI to XII)

3. that in order to divert students to different
    vocations after 10 to 12 years of schooling,
    a large number of occupational institutes
    be open;

4. that refresher courses be organized by the
    universities for high school and intermediate
    college teachers;

5. that to avoid overcrowding at universities
    and colleges, the maximum number in the Arts
    and Science faculties of a teaching university
    be fixed at 3,000 and in an affiliated college
    at 1,500;

6. that the number of working days be substan-
    tially increased to ensure a minimum of 180
    in the year, exclusive of examination days;
    with three terms, each of about 11 weeks'
    duration;

7. that lectures be carefully planned and supple-
    mented by tutorials, library work and written
    exercises;

8. that there be no prescribed textbooks for
    any courses of study;

9. that attendance at lectures be compulsory
    for undergraduate students as at present,
    and that private candidates of only certain
    categories be allowed to appear for public
    examinations. An experiment should, however,
    be made with evening colleges for working
    people;

10. that tutorial instruction be developed in
    all institutions imparting university education
    in the following manner:

    a. students should report to tutors in groups
        not exceeding 6 in number;

    b. tutorials should be made available to
        all under-graduates, both pass and honors;

c. tutorials should stimulate the mental development of students and should not become mere coaching for examinations;

d. if tutorials are to succeed, the teaching staff should be improved in quality and quantity.

11. that university libraries be greatly improved by:

a. larger annual grants;

b. the introduction of the open access system;

c. longer hours of work;

d. better organization; and

e. a well-trained staff which should include reference assistants;

12. that the laboratories be improved in building, fittings equipment, workshops and technicians.[18]

Thus, it has been noted that the University Education Commission (1948-49) has considered practically every aspect of university education: aims of university education, structure and administration, admission policies, teaching and examination, courses of study (general and professional), research, medium of instruction, teachers and their conditions of service, student and discipline, residential halls, student service, finance, buildings, libraries, laboratories, and other miscellaneous aspects. Though all recommendations could not be carried out, every attempt has been made in implementing them within the limit of the available resources. It was in accordance with the recommendations of this Commission that the University Grants Commission was established to coordinate and determine standards in the institutions of higher education.

University Education Commission (1966 Report)

M. C. Chagla, former Education Minister of the Central (Federal) Government of India, and former Indian Ambassador to the United States, appointed an Education Commission in July 1964, under the chairmanship of Dr. D. S. Kothari, Chairman of the University Grants Commission, and composed of 11 Indian and 5 foreign members

(two from England and one each from United States, Japan,
France and the Union of the Soviet Socialist Republics).
The Commission's task was to make a thorough evaluation
of current and future education with emphasis on the
roots of Indian culture and civilization and the need
to develop education along scientific lines. The specific
assignment was to survey the entire field of Education
in India and then recommend to the Government national
education patterns, principles, and policies to aid
the development of education at all stages and in all
fields except medical and legal.[19]

This Commission stated that "education should be
developed so as to increase productivity, achieve social
and national integration, strengthen democracy, accelerate the process of modernization and cultivate social,
moral and spiritual values."[20]

The report defines the function of universities
as follows:

> ... to seek and cultivate new
> knowledge, to engage vigorously
> and fearlessly in the pursuit
> of truth, and to interpret old
> knowledge and beliefs in the light
> of new needsand discoveries; to
> provide the right kind of leader-
> ship in all walk of life, to
> identify gifted youth and help
> them develop their potential to
> the full by cultivation of physical
> fitness, developing the powers
> of the mind and cultivation of
> right interests, attitudes and
> moral and intellectual values;
> to provide society with competent
> men and women trained in agricul-
> ture, art, medicine, science and
> technology and various other profes-
> sions, who will also be cultivated
> individuals imbued with a sense
> of social purpose; to strive to
> promote equality and social justice
> and to reduce social and cultural
> differences through diffusion of
> education; and to foster in the
> teachers and students, and through

48

them in society generally, the
attitudes and values needed for
developing the good life in individuals and society.[21]

The report further recommended that Indian universities should perform two specific functions: (1) develop university extension by correspondence course
and in-service education programmes for professional
workers of all kinds, and by general adult education
programmes and improve education through courses, institutes, and the development of new curricula, textbooks,
and teaching materials.[22]

The report of the Education Commission published
in June 1966, is perhaps another landmark in the history
of education in India. The report has been widely commented upon by all concerned. The Government of India,
after examining all its aspects, recommended it to
Parliament for its approval. Accordingly, the "Report
on National Policy on Higher Education" was presented
to the Parliament on July 25, 1967. It was recommended
that:

> The duration of the academic
> course at the higher secondary
> state (or the pre-university)
> should be uniformly raised to
> two years in all parts of the
> country under a phased plan.
> The curriculum should include
> two languages, three subjects
> selected from a prescribed list,
> work-experience and social ser-
> vice, physical and health edu-
> cation, and education in moral
> and social values. The academic
> control of this stage should be
> entrusted to a single authority
> in each State on which the uni-
> versities should have adequate
> representation.
>
> The duration of the vocational
> courses at this stage should vary
> according to their objectives
> (1-3 years). They should cover
> a larger number of fields such

as agriculture, industry, trade
and commerce, medicine and public
health, home management, arts
and crafts, education, secretariat
training.

Education at this stage should
be largely terminal so that a
majority of students who complete
class XII[23]enter different walks
of life.

It was further pointed out that the duration of
the courses for the first degree in arts, science and
commerce should be three years after the higher secondary
stage. At the university stage, it was recommended
that immediate and effective steps be taken to reorganize courses and to revise and upgrade curriculum.
The report urged that the link between the subjects
taken at the school stage and those at the first degree
should be less rigid and combinations of subjects permissible for the first and the second degrees should
be more elastic than was generally the case. Special
efforts necessary to promote inter-disciplinary studies
were recommended and the university was called on to
define the admission requirements to different courses
of study at the undergraduate level and allow ineligible
students to reappear at the relevant examination to
earn eligibility. Similarly, the report said that the
number of students to be admitted to each college or
department of university should be determined according
to the availability of teachers and facilities. However,
adequate resources should be provided for all the eligible students to gain admission to higher education.
Also some allowances for the handicapped students from
rural areas, urban slums and from the weaker sections[24]
of the community were urged.

Thus the 1964-66 Education Commission, consisting
of some of the most distinguished Indian educationists
and experts from a number of foreign countries, was
another impressive and comprehensive report on university
education. It attempted to explore the existing system
of education at all levels (except medical and legal)
-- primary, secondary, and higher education -- and to
make suggestions to improve the system. That this
Commission has been concerned with all levels of education is seen from the following passage found in the

foreword to the report:

> The need to bring about a major
> improvement in the effectiveness
> of primary education; to introduce
> work-experience as an integral
> element of general education;
> to vocationalize secondary edu-
> cation; to improve the quality
> of teachers at all levels and
> to provide teachers in sufficient
> strength; to liquidate illiteracy;
> to strengthen centres of advanced
> study and strive to attain, in
> some of our universities at least,
> higher international standards;
> to lay special emphasis on the
> combination of teaching and re-
> search and to pay particular
> attention to education and re-
> search in agriculture and allied
> sciences.[25]

The Commission recommended that resources be
concentrated on the problems enumerated in the above
paragraph. But the question is: Does India have
enough resources to implement these schemes? Since
money is very limited and personnel with the ability
and experience is scarce, implementation has been
rather slow.

The University Grants Commission

In pursuance of the recommendations of the University Education Commission, the University Grants Commission (UGC) was set up in 1953. Article 5 of the UGC
Act says that:

1. The commission shall consist of 9 members
    to be appointed by the Central Government.

2. The members shall be chosen as follows:

    a. Not more than 3 members from among
        the Vice-Chancellors of Universities.

    b. two members from the officers of the
        Central Government; and

51

c. the remaining numbers from among persons
    who are educationists of repute or
    who have obtained high academic distinc-
    tions, provided that not less than
    one-half of the total number so chosen
    shall be from among persons who are
    not officers of the Central Government
    or of any State Government.

3. The Central Government shall nominate a
    member of the commission, not being an officer
    of the Central Government or of any State
    Government to be the Chairman thereof.[26]

The Act also provides that "office of the Chairman
shall be a whole time and salaried one, and every
member shall unless he becomes disqualified for continuing as such, hold office for a period of six year."[27]

The University Grants Commission was formally
inaugurated in New Delhi by Maulana Abdul Kalum Azard,
who was the Education Minister, on December 28, 1953.
Prime Minister Nehru was also present and addressed
the inaugural meeting. The functions of the Commission
were:

1. to advise Government on the allocation of
    grants-in-aid from public funds to central
    universities.

2. to advise Government on the allocation of
    grants-in-aid to other universities and
    institutions of higher learning whose case
    for such grants may be referred to the Com-
    mission by Government; and

3. to advise the universities and other institu-
    tions of higher learning with respect to
    any question referred by the Government
    to the Commission.[28]

The first Chairman of the Commission in 1953,
Dr. Shanti Swarul Bhatnagar, held the post of Chairman
along with that of Secretary to the Government of
India in the Ministry of Natural Resources and Scientific Research. Dr. Bhatnagar died on January 1, 1955.
Shortly afterward, Shri Humayun Kabir, then Secretary
to the Government of India in the Ministry of Education,

was appointed to act as Chairman of the Commission in addition to his other duties. Sri Kabir resigned on February 22, 1956. Pandit Hridaynath Kunzru, Member of the Parliament, temporarily acted as Chairman until August 28, 1956, when Dr. C. D. Deshmukh, formerly Finance Minister of India, was appointed Chairman.[29]

The first three Chairmen of the Commission acted in an honorary capacity and the fourth Chairman, Dr. C. D. Deshmukh, since his appointment has been working on a nominal salary of Rs. 1/per month. This has saved the Commission a sum of about Rs. 36,000 annually.[30]

The Chairman of the Commission should not be an officer of the Central Government or a State Government and should be nominated by the Central Government. The office of Chairman is a whole-time and salaried one. Dr. C. D. Deshmukh was the first whole-time Chairman of the University Grants Commission.[31]

The University Grants Commission Act, which was passed by the Parliament, stated that the Commission may:

a. enquire into the financial needs of Universities;

b. allocate and disburse, out of the Fund of the Commission grants to Universities established or incorporated by or under a Central Act for the maintenance and development of such universities or for any general or special purpose;

c. allocate and disburse, out of the Fund of the Commission, such grants to other Universities as it may deem necessary for the development of such Universities or for any other general or specified purpose: Provided that in making any grant to any such University, the Commission shall give due consideration to the development of the University concerned, its financial needs, the standard attained by it and the national purposes which it may serve;

d. recommend to any university the measures necessary for the improvement of University education and advise the university upon

53

the action to be taken for the purpose of implementing such recommendation;

e. advise the Central Government or any State Government on the allocation of any grants to Universities for any general for specified purpose out of the Consolidated Fund or the State, as case may be;

f. advise any authority, if such advice is asked for, on the establishment of a new university or proposals connected with the expansion of the activities of any University;

g. advise the Central Government or any State Government or University on any question which may be referred to the Commission by the Central Government or the State Government or the University, as the case may be;

h. Collect information on all such matters relating to university education in India and other countries as it thinks fit and make the same available to any universities;

i. require a University to furnish it with such information as may be needed relating to the financial position of the University or the studies in the various branches of learning undertaken in that university, together with all the rules and regulations relating to the standards of teaching and examination in that university respecting such branches of learning; and

j. perform such other functions as may be prescribed or as may be deemed necessary by the Commission for Advancing the cause of higher education in India or as may be incidental or conductive to the discharge of the above functions.[32]

The Commission also provides funds for various developmental programmes in the field of higher education:

The Commission provides funds for various developmental programmes, through grants for building up libraries, laboratories, hostels, non-resident student centres, hobby workshops, centres of advanced study in various fields of knowledge, development of post-graduate research, etc. In addition, the improvement of salary scales of teachers, encouragement of science education measures for promotion of general education courses, organizing conferences, seminars, summer schools and refresher courses, construction of staff quarters, staff clubs and guest houses, travel grants research fellowships and scholarships, etc., are some of the schemes which the Commission assists.[33]

In 1970, the Lok Sabha passed a UGC amendment Bill. It provides the enlargement of membership of the University Grants Commission from 9 to 12, up to three of them on a full time basis. Serving Vice-Chancellors and the heads of the institutions eligible for UGC grants would not be permitted to become the members of the Commission.

Of the three full time members, one would be responsible for student welfare and will look into the various student's problems. The second would be in charge of the affairs of colleges which are assisted by or seeking assistance from the Commission. The third will hold the responsibility of the follow-up work on the recommendations of Education Commission regarding its implementation, etc. Of the remaining nine, two would be the officials of the Central Government, five would be selected from among business men, industries, educationists and from other professions.[34]

55

This enlargement of membership from 9 to 12 is desirable, especially the provision for three full-time personnel for the welfare of students' affairs, affairs of the colleges, and for the co-ordination and implementation of the recommendation of the Commission. Full time Commissioners are able to devote more time for the development and improvement of higher educational programmes. Selection of members from business, industries, education and from other professions is also desirable, for it allows for more representation from the public and less control by the Government.

Suraj Bhan, former Vice-Chancellor of the Punjab University summarized the accomplishments of the University Grants Commission in the following words:

> . . . This multifaceted improvement programme of the Commission has brought about cataclysmic changes in the nature, functions and shape of the Indian universities, and has resulted in the expansion of higher education, provision of better laboratories and libraries, multiplicity and enrichment of academic offerings, stepping-up of standards of teaching and research, insuring a fair and proper deal to students and sponsoring of several schemes to raise the esteem and status of teachers.[35]

As had been noted, apart from the assistance it gives for raising the standards of teaching and research, the Commission has been providing grants for special projects such as the introduction of general education courses in the universities, examination reform, publication of doctoral thesis, etc. It has also been providing funds for various developmental programmes such as libraries, laboratories, hostels, non-residential student centres, and in the development of post-graduate research. Other schemes which have been fostered by the Commission are: construction of staff quarters, staff clubs and guest houses, travel grants, research fellowships and scholarships, the improvement of salary scales of teachers, encouragement

of science education, etc. Thus the University Grants
Commission is the single governmental agency responsible
for the planning, coordination, and administration
of higher education in India on a national level.
It is an expert body with the power to allocate grants
instead of merely recommending them to the Finance
Ministry.

The activities of the University Grants Commission
(like that of the United Grants Committee of the United
Kingdom) are not subject to frequent and detailed
scrutiny by Government. However, there are certain
differences between the two bodies due to the differences
in the administrative systems of the two countries.
While the University Grants Committee in the United
Kingdom deals with the financial needs of all the
universities in the same way, in India only five (centrally administered) universities are the direct and
complete responsibility of the University Grants Commission. The other universities (state-controlled)
are only partially dependent on the University Grants
Commission for funds. Their respective State Governments give them financial assistance.[36]

The actual working of the University Grants Commission may be summarized as follows: (1) Promotion
and coordination of higher education and the maintenance
of university education, (2) to appropriate and disburse
out of its funds grants to the five centrally administered universities for their development and maintenance,
(3) to advise the central and states governments concerning the establishment of new universities, the
allocation of grants, and the expansion of the activities
of existing universities, (4) to enquire into the
financial needs of all other universities and make
grants to them for development, (5) to collect information from and on behalf of the universities.

The Five-Year Plans

The Five-Year Plans have also emphasized that
education is vitally important to the success of India's
self-government and to the attainment of her national
goals.

First and Second Five-Year Plans (1951-56, 1956-61)

"In a democratic set-up the role of education
becomes crucial, since it can function effectively

only if there is an intelligent participation of the masses in the affairs of the country."[37]

"The system of education in a country has a determining influence on the rate at which economic progress is achieved and benefits which can be derived from it."[38]

The Planning Commission was set up in March 1950 soon after Independence, to formulate development plans for the country as a whole. The draft of the First-Five Year Plan was published in July 1951 and it was approved by Parliament in December 1952.

> The first Five Year Plan (1951-52 to 1955-56), through its emphasis on agriculture, irrigation, power and transport, aimed at creation of the base for more rapid economic and industrial advance in the future. It also initiated some of the basic policies by way of social change and institutional reforms. The Second Plan (1956-57 to 1960-61)carried these policies a step further and placed before the nation the goal of a socialist pattern of society.[39]

The Second-Five Year Plan (1956-61) allocated twice as much to education as did the first plan. To higher education alone, the financial allocation was four times as much.[40] Real efforts were made to improve the liberal arts colleges by putting more stress upon equality than expansion. The rapid enrollment increase (almost 80 percent) in the arts and science colleges had brought serious overcrowing and a lowering of standards because the staff and facilities could not expand fast enough to keep pace.[41]

The Second Plan also included provision for seven new universities and for building new libraries, laboratories, and hostels (residence halls) for existing colleges. Research scholarships and an urgently needed increase in faculty salaries were also proposed.[42]

In connection with the Second National Five-Year Plan (1956-61) the Planning Commission of the Government

58

of India made an allocation of 27 crores of rupees
to the University Grants Commission for the "development"
of the Universities. (This amount excludes the sums
required for "maintenance" grants to the Central Universities.)[43]

Third five year plan (1961-66)

Third Five Year Plan placed great emphasis upon
the education of the country. The following passage
makes this fact clear:

> Education is the most important
> single factor in achieving rapid
> economic development and tech-
> nological progress and in creating
> social order founded on the values
> of freedom, social justice, and
> equal opportunity. . . . In all
> branches of national life, ed-
> ucation becomes the focal point
> of planned development. . . .
> At all stages of education the
> aim must be to develop both skill
> and knowledge and a creative
> outlook, a feeling of national
> unity which stands above religion,
> caste, and language, and an un-
> derstanding of common interests
> and obligations.[44]

There has been marked progress in the spread
of education both general and technical during the
period of the third five-year plan. The Constitutional directive regarding free and compulsory education up to the age of 14 has not been fulfilled as
planned. There was marked progress in school enrollment and eight out of ten children of 6-11 years of
age have been attending school. "The rapid spread
of facilities for secondary and higher education has
been mainly responsible for facilitating vertical
mobility of labour. Technical and engineering courses
have been widely introduced; there are 138 colleges
of engineering besides 284 institutions for diploma
courses. About a sixth of students attending colleges
receive scholarships and stipends."[45]

Fourth five-year plan (1969-74)

The approach to education during the Fourth Five-Year Plan period is three-fold: (1) to remove the present deficiencies in the system and link it more purposefully to social and economic development of the country, (2) to improve standards and quality at all stages and (3) to extend educational facilities to meet social urges and economic needs.[46]

The final document of Fourth Five-Year Plan was presented to the parliament on May 18, 1970 by the Prime Minister Mrs. Indira Gandhi "The plan with an outlay of Rs. 248,820 Million ($33,176 Million), has equality with social justice and the care of the common man, weak and underprivileged, as its dominant theme."[47] In this finalized fourth Five-Year Plan, "education has been allocated a sum of Rs. 8,490 Million or 5.8 percent of the total plan outlay."[48]

Fifth five-year plan (1975-1980)

Broadly speaking, the Fifth Plan laid emphasis on (1) ensuring equality of educational opportunities as part of the overall plan of ensuring social justice; (2) establishing closer links between the pattern of education on the one hand and the needs of development and the employment market, on the other; (3) improvement of the quality of education imparted and (4) involvement of the academic community, including students, in the tasks of social and economic development.[49]

Sixth five-year plan (1980-1985)

The Sixth Year Plan lays emphasis on (1) programmes of adult education including eradication of adult illiteracy. (2) universalization of elementary education; (3) vocationalisation at the secondary stage and improvement of quality in the secondary stage and higher education; (4) better and more effective utilization on non-plan government expenditure for meeting developmental goals; (5) improvement of the quality and implementation of educational programmes in states where universalisation of elementary education has made lesser headway and the prevalence of illiteracy among adults remains large; and (6) ensuring a rural bias in the educational programmes, to develop science education and scientific attitude and to provide a

60

system of non-formal education and training at all stages.[56]

Thus the Five-Year Plans allocated millions of rupees for the development of higher education. It helped to open many universities, and provided building facilities for the existing universities. So the six Five-Year Plans have contributed much to the advancement of higher education of India.

The State Government educational organization

As it was noted in the third chapter of this paper, the main responsibility for education rests with State Governments. The State legislatures must pass enabling acts to start new universities, and State Governments are a major source of revenue for all educational levels.

The organization and administration of educational system varies from State to State. However, the basic structure has undergone little change over the last 35 years, since independence.

In every State there is an Education Minister at the apex assisted by an Education Secretary. In some States there is also a Deputy Minister of Education. The Department of Education has two main organs: (1) the Secretariat, which has a policy-making and coordination function, and (2) the directorate of education which performs the functions of direction, regulation and inspection.

The directorate of education which is the 'hard core' of the machinery of educational administration in each State has developed a tendency in recent years to be concerned mainly with the school level of education. The establishment of independent directorates of collegiate and technical education is another recent trend noticeable in some States.

61

In some States, technical education is administered by the
Department of Industry; in others,[51]
by the public work Department.

The great increase of educational activity during
the last 35 years has brought about not only an expansion in the size and complexity of the State education
organization but also in several important new developments. Some States have:

1. Passed laws making primary and secondary
   education compulsory.

2. Established boards for secondary education.

3. Initiated school service related to audio-
   visual aids, curriculum planning, evaluation,
   guidance, textbooks, and other matters.

4. Established advisory bodies on education,
   with both official and unofficial representation.

4. Decentralized the supervising and inspection
   functions of State education departments
   to district officers and inspectors.

6. Increased local control and support of primary
   education, consistent with a national effort
   to organize, strengthen, and stimulate local
   self-government.[52]

The 1966 Education Commission also made several
recommendations on State education organization.
The important ones are as follows:

I. Reorganize their education departments to:

   1. Develop and implement a program of
      school improvement.

   2. Prescribe and enforce standards.

   3. Provide and train teachers.

   4. Take responsibility for inspection and
      revitalized supervision of schools.

62

5. Provide extension service.

6. Coordinate secondary vocational and technical education.

II. Establish State institutes of education:

1. Provide in-service training for department staff.

2. Improve teacher education.

3. Improve textbooks, guidance programs, and research and evaluation programs.

III. Establish an autonomous State Evaluation Organization.

IV. Establish State boards of school education with board powers to supervise all primary and secondary education, including external examinations at the end of the lower and higher secondary stage.

V. Establish a National Board of School Education in the Central (Federal) Ministry of Education to advise the Central Government on all elementary and secondary education. Such a board should define, revise, and evaluate standards at all levels, advise State education departments and college with universities and University Grants Commission.[53]

External organization and administration of State Government with regard to the universities and colleges is similar from state to state, although variations have increased with individual efforts to develop higher education level rapidly. The typical organization structure is usually divided into a small secretariat, or directorate of education, which serves as a policy and making and coordinating agency. They are responsible for supervising, regulating and inspecting institutions. They have a kind of centralized control with regards to the curriculum, textbooks, examinations and standards.

For example, in the State of Kerala, the education is under the control of the ministry and its secretariat.

Under the state ministry of education, there is a directorate or direcor of public instruction to administer all the activities of the school system such as inspection, curriculum textbooks, examinations and standards, promotion and appointment of teachers, etc. The Director of Education is the permanent head of the Education, and he also acts as the technical adviser to the Minister of Education. Under the Director of Public Instructors, there are District Educational Officers and their deputies to supervise the educational activities in their respective districts. Next to the Director of Public Instructors are the regional inspectors. While they are mainly in charge of secondary schools and training institutions for primary teachers, the regional inspectors exercise general supervision over all educational activities within their jurisdiction. With regard to higher education in Kerala, all affiliated colleges are under the direct control of the three universities. The universities are directly under the control of the ministry of Kerala and its secretariat. The Governor is the honorary head of the university; the Education Minister is repsonsible to the state legislators.

The 1948-49 Commission stressed the evil of absolute State control over education. "Exclusive control of education by the State has been an important factor in facilitating the maintenance of totalitarian tyrannies," noted the Commission.[54]

Dr. D. D. Tewari, former principal of the Government Central Pedagogical Institute, Allahabad, emphasized "decentralization" in India's future educational planning. He stated that, in a democratic society, the people should look to themselves to share the responsibility in educational development instead of looking to the Government alone for all that ought to be done. The goals of education must be realized through the initiative of teachers and the local community. Decentralization in education implies people's participation in educational development and full functional freedom to the school and the teacher. Leadership in the field of education should not belong to government; rather, it should be for the professional organizations of teachers to provide effective leadership in the field of education. This leadership must be built up from the base. It should lay down the educational policy of the country, give guidelines for

the curriculum, text books, methods of teaching and
evaluation.[55]

In India, the State control over the institutions
of higher learning is too rigid. Even a local community
or private instituion does not have the power or freedom to start a college unless it gets prior approval
from the State Government. All the universities are
controlled either by the State or Central Government
and they are financed by these governments for the
most part. Such exclusive control is not conducive
to individual development; further, such rigid control
makes it difficult for the private and independent
institutions of higher learning to keep pace with
the changing demands of the time. In order to meet
the challenge of modern educational trends, each
college should be given the power and freedom to establish its own departments, to conduct its own examinations,
and grant its own degree at least at the undergraduate
level.

The Philathropic and Religious Organization

Private voluntary organizations have played a
great role in the field of higher education. Large
numbers of colleges are organized and administered
by private religious organizations. They receive
aid from the State and Central Government. Regarding
this, the **1966 Report** of the Education Commission
points out:

> It should be an objective of
> educational policy to encourage
> and to make full use of all assis-
> tance that can come through the
> voluntary efforts of the people.

> The policy of the Government
> towards schools conducted by
> voluntary organizations should
> be selective rather than uniform.
> The system of grants-in-aid should
> be revised, simplified and made
> more liberal. All recognized
> schools should be eligible for
> grants-in-aid on some egalitarian
> basis which will help them to
> maintain proper standards. In

addition, there should be provision for penal cuts for gross
failure or special grants for
good and outstanding work.[56]

In the Report of the Committee Members of Parliament on Education the same thought was expressed.
The voluntary organizations have played a very important
role in the development of education in the past.
In the days ahead, they can make valuable contributions
at the primary, secondary and university stages.
Therefore it should be an objective of education policy
to encourage and to make full use of all the assistance
that can come through the voluntary efforts of the
people in the country.[57] The number of colleges according to type of management we present in Table 1.

Even though the provision was provided by the
Central Government to encourage voluntary organizations,
they do not enjoy full autonomy in the external and
internal administration of higher education. Since
the State and Central Government finance the private
colleges to a large extent, the colleges have the
same responsibilities and privileges as the Government
colleges. However, they enjoy certain measures of
autonomy in their internal administration.

Internal Organization and Administration

of Higher Education

The internal organization and administration of
the first three universities -- Calcutta, Bombay and
Madras -- started in 1857, and many subsequent Indian
universities was patterned after that of the University
of London. In both England and India, however, the
organizational pattern has varied at times, although
essentially it remains the same. The officers and
governing bodies of Indian universities have the same
names, titles and responsibilities in each university.

TABLE 1 [58]

NUMBER OF COLLEGES ACCORDING TO TYPES OF MANAGEMENT:

1961-62 to 1967-68

Year	University Colleges	Private Colleges	Government Colleges	Total Number of Colleges	Increase in Number of Colleges Over The Preceding Year
1961-62	107	1,223	453	1,783	241
1962-63	133	1,333	472	1,938	155
1963-64	128	1,485	498	2,111	173
1964-65	147	1,686	527	2,360	219
1965-66	163	1,841	518	2,572	212
1966-67	166	1,968	615	2,749	177

Organizational Structure and Administration

of the Universities

In India there are four main types of universities.
They are: (1) teaching and affiliating, (2) unitary
teaching, (3) purely affiliating, and (4) federal
teaching. The majority of them belong to teaching
and affiliating type, that is, they carry on teaching
activities in their own departments and or through
constituent colleges, and instruction is given either
by their own teachers or constituent colleges recognized by them. They also affiliate colleges within
their jurisdiction which teach under university supervision.

These colleges have to abide by their conditions
of affiliation with regard to finance, adequacy of
staff, equipment, libraries, laboratories, buildings
and hostels. In some universities falling in this
category, the central core predominates, as in Andhra
University and in Poona University; in others, the
affiliated colleges do most of the teaching, the university's teaching being restricted to a few departments.[59]

The unitary teaching university is another type
of Indian university. There are twenty-one such universities in India. A unitary teaching university has
been defined as "one, usually localized in a single
centre, in which the whole of the teaching is conducted
by teachers appointed by or under the control of the
university. The control of the teachers, the teaching,
the courses of study and the administration are centralized in the university. Usually, a unitary teaching
university is residential, and vice versa. The universities which conform to this type are: Allahabad,
Annamalai, Banaras, Baroda, Jadavapur, Kurushetra,
Lucknow, Patna, Roorkee and Visva Bharati.

Most of the Indian universities began as affiliating universities, learning mainly concerned with laying
down courses of study and examining students sent
up by their colleges. These universities had no control
over the teaching imparted in the affiliated colleges
and were practically no more than external, examining
bodies. Gradually, these universities began to assume
teaching functions and associated their teachers with
the framing of courses and their general administration.

There is only one purely affiliated university in India today and that is Agra University.[60]

The universities of Bombay, Kerala and Bangalore are federal teaching universities. Its colleges are affiliated colleges and enjoy a great measure of autonomy in their internal administration, but they can be required to pool their resources for both post-graduate and post-intermediate teaching. Their principals are ex-officio members of the senate, the academic council and boards of university teaching, and the heads of their departments are ex-officio members of the university's boards of studies. Thus, there is a close link between the university and the colleges. Poona University is a federal teaching university as far as the Poona area is concerned, though it is an affiliated university in relation to the colleges situated outside Poona.[61]

Though there are four types of universities in India, the organization and administration of all these types of universities are almost the same. The organization and administration of the various types of universities will not be discussed separately.

The chief officers and governing bodies of Indian universities usually have the same names, titles, and responsibilities in each university. The chief officers of an Indian university are: (1) the Chancellor, (2) the Vice-Chancellor, (3) the Registrar, (4) the Bursar, and (5) the Visitor.

The Chancellor

The Chancellor or the head of the university is, as a general rule, the governor of the State. It is an honorary office. He presides at the senate meetings and also at any convocation at the university.

> Present practice varies but in
> most provincial universities the
> Governor of the Province is ex-
> officio Chancellor. This arrangement
> has worked well, especially in
> provinces with only one universi-
> ty. Where there are several uni-
> versities in one Province the
> Governor himself may feel that

he cannot give to all of them
as much personal contact as
is desirable. This a question
which should be settled by each
Province (or State) for itself.[62]

The Chancellor of the university, generally,
appoints the Vice-Chancellor form a panel of names
which has been submitted by the supreme governing
body of the university (senate). His duties are similar
to that of the Chairman of the Board of Trustees in
the American university. The State Governor-Chancellor
is usually the ceremonial head of the university, with
power to approve or veto the appointment of a Vice-
Chancellor (he seldom vetos a duly chosen person).
In addition to performing ceremonial duties, the Chancellor may assist in settling conflicts between various
authorities of the universities.

The Vice Chancellor

The chief academic and executive officer of the
university is the Vice-Chancellor, who is a full-time,
paid officer, in most of the Indian universities.
He is appointed by the Chancellor, who selects him
from among the candidates proposed by the supreme
governing body of the university. "He is usually
a full-time paid officer appointed for a fixed term
by the Chancellor from a panel of names submitted
to him by the Senate or Court. (In some universities
such as Bombay, Poona, Gujart and Baroda the post
of Vice-Chancellor is an honorary one.)"[63]

The Report of the University Education Commission
states:

Originally the Vice-Chancellorship
of an Indian university was regarded as an honorary post to
be filled by a prominent man in
his leisure time. If he had academic interests, so much the better;
but sometimes he had not. A Vice-
Chancellor coming in from outside
and holding office for two or
three years could not become
intimately acquainted with the
details of administration or with

70

the personnel of the university.

While the universities were solely
or mainly affiliation, this conception of the Vice-Chancellor's
office was quite natural, and
in fact, there was not enough
work to justify a full-time appointment. But now the position has
changed. There are numerous unitary, teaching universities and
most of the "affiliating" universities have added teaching and
research to their functions, in
some instances on a very large
and complex scale. Elsewhere
we have strongly urged that the
purely affiliation university
is ineffective and obsolete in
conception and should be abolished.
It is not surprising therefore
that the overwhelming mass of
opinion offered to us recommends
that all universities should in
future have full-time, paid Vice-
Chancellors. . . .[64]

The duties of the Vice-Chancellor are many.
In the absence of the Chancellor he presides over
the court (senate), syndicate, academic council, and
numerous committees including the selection committee
for the appointment of the staff. It is his duty
to know the senior members of the staff intimately,
and to be known to all the members of the staff and
students. By adequate academic reputation and by
strength of personality, he must command the confi-
dence of the staff and students. "He must know his
university well enough to be able to foster its points
of strength and to foresee possible points of weakness
before they become acute."[65]

The Vice-Chancellor must be the keeper of the
university's conscience, both setting the highest
standard by example and dealing promptly and firmly
with indiscipline or malpractice of any kind. As
a constitutional ruler, he is required to do all these
without using autocratic power. He also has to act
as the chief liaison between his university and the

71

public. It is his duty to keep the university alive
to the duties it owes to the public and to win support
for the university and understanding of its needs
not merely from potential benefactors but from the
general public and its elected representatives. He
must have the strength of character to resist unflinch-
ingly the many forms of pressure to relax standards
of all sorts, which are being applied to universities
today. It is a full-time task and it needs an excep-
tional man to undertake it.[66]

It was also recommended that certain safeguards
in the method of choosing the Vice-Chancellor be laid
down by each university in its Statutes:

1. The Chancellor should appoint the Vice-Chancel-
    lor upon the recommendation of the executive
    council of the university.

2. The executive council should send forward
    one name only to Chancellor. He can of
    course refer the name back but cannot initiate
    the appointment himself.

3. The executive council should be charged
    to maintain strict privacy in their delibera-
    tions concerning the appointment. No doubt
    there may be differences of opinion and
    actual voting inside the executive council
    but they must keep this to themselves until
    they emerge with the name of the man whom
    they are requesting the Chancellor to appoint.
    There is of course no objection to their
    privately approaching the man of their choice
    to see if he is willing to serve, before
    they send his name forward to the Chancellor.

4. The whole idea of "standing as a candidate"
    for the Vice-Chancellorship must be suppressed.
    The executive council must in no way be
    limited to considering the names of would
    be candidates. On the contrary, they should
    regard a man's declared intention of seeking
    the Vice-Chancellorship as prima facie evidence
    of his unfitness for the post.[67]

About the tenure of the office of the Vice-Chancellor, the Education Commission unanimously recommended

72

that "all Vice-Chancellors should be appointed for
six years and should not be eligible for reelection."[68]
This is a good recommendation because this long tenure
period of six years gives him ample time to plan and
implement the educational programmes in an effective
way.

In the Indian universities, the Vice-Chancellor
is generally responsible for the entire administration
of the university. All other officers and personnel
are delegated their responsibility by the Vice-Chancellor.
Thus the university affairs are mainly the responsibility
of the Vice-Chancellor.

The Registrar

The registrar is a full-time salaried officer,
appointed by the syndicate for a probationary period
of two years. He is usually the custodian of the
building facilities, libraries, records, and other
properties of the university. He acts as the secretary
of the senate, the syndicate, and other university
committees. He is responsible for keeping minutes
of their meetings, for issuing notices and official
correspondence of the university affairs. Haggerty
stated: Having relatively long tenure, the registrar
has wide-ranging responsibility for the daily and
detailed academic administration, thus providing the
continuity necessary for efficient operation of the
university."[69]

The Bursar (Treasurer)

The bursar is also a full-time salaried officer
who is directly responsible to the Vice-Chancellor
in the financial affairs of a university. He is the
custodian of the money matters, with regard to the
students--tuition fees, paying of salary to faculty
and other university personnel, and the day-to-day
financial affairs of the university. He prepares
the budget and keeps the vouchers and receipts of
all income and expenditure. He is also responsible
for the internal audit of the university.

The Visitor

Before Independence the title of the visitor
was very common in the universities of India as in
the British universities. The University Education

Commission states that "The Governor-General (or president if the head of the state is to be known by that
title) should be the Visitor of all universities in
India, as he was until 1937." [96]

Since Independence all the provinces have been
changed to states and now there are twenty-two states
in India. The head of the state is known as the Governor,
so the Governor is the honorary Chancellor of the
respective state universities. Thus, the term "visitor"
does not exist in the universities of India except
in the central universities and a few institutes.
Haggerty pointed out that in the Indian Institutes
of Technology, the Indian Institute of Science, and
in the Central Universities, the President of India
holds the title of 'visitor' in an ex-officio capacity." [71]

In addition to the officers just described, most
Indian universities also have deans of faculties and
department heads, librarians, rector and in a few
universities an honorary Pro-Chancellor and Pro-Vice-
Chancellor for the effective administration. Figure
2 will explain the organizational structure of a typical
university in India.

In summary, for the effective governing of universities and colleges in India, more and more participation
of faculty, students, administrators, alumni, parents,
community, outstanding educationists, legislators,
the government--both state and federal--should be
encouraged. This means more participation by all
the constituencies of the university, the community,
and the government agencies. This also means less
control of the government and more autonomy in their
internal and external administration of the institutions
of higher learning.

University Organization and Administration

Since there are a great many kinds of tasks to
be performed and since the whole hierarchy of officials
has to be appointed in the organized governmental
activities of modern time, one tends to think of administration in any context as wielding authority and
keeping things under control. Administration in its
simplest and basic sense means only carrying out the
duties assigned to a functionary and making it possible
for an institution or organization to carry out the
functions assigned to it. Samuel Mathai states:

74

I. UNIVERSITY OFFICERS

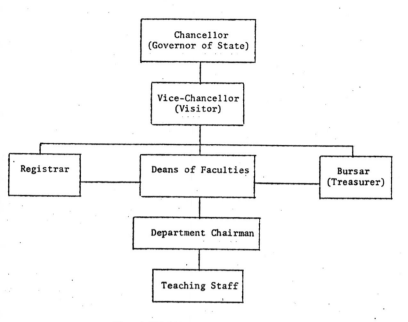

II. ADMINISTRATIVE AUTHORITIES

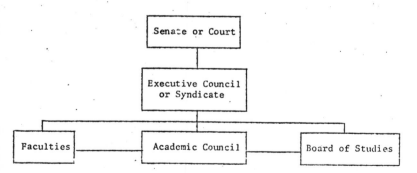

Prepared by: N. Koshy Samuel

Figure 1.   Organizational structure of a typical university in India.

> In the field of education the
> primary business of institutions
> is to make possible the nurture
> and training of children and older
> persons and therefore educational
> administration should mean the
> machinery required for the efficient
> functioning of schools and colleges
> and universities. Efficient func-
> tioning involves many different
> kinds of separate activities,
> and good educational administration
> is that which takes care of all
> the various aspects of the life
> of an educational institution.
> . . . A university in the modern
> world has to have a close and
> vital relation with society at
> large, and the administration
> of a university should embody
> this concern in a suitable manner.[72]

Though there is considerable variation in the
administration of different universities, in general
the pattern of administration is the same. The main
bodies of administration and their relationship to
one another follows more or less the same pattern,
with minor differences. Each university has at least
four governing bodies: (1) the senate or the court,
(2) the syndicate or executive council, (3) the academic
council and (4) the faculties. In some universities
there are also finance committees, boards of studies,
selection committees, boards of post-graduate studies
and or research, boards of inspection and board of
university teaching.

The Senate or Court

The Indian universities have had two main governing
and advisory councils as authorities of the university
ever since 1857 when the first universities were established. One of them is the senate or court. The
other is the syndicate executive council which is
a relatively small body. The senate is the supreme
governing body of a university, which decides broad
questions of policy. It has the power to review the
actions of the other authorities.

76

Regarding the members of the senate, Mathai states:

The senates of many of our universities frequently include persons
whose knowledge of the needs,
and problems of modern university
is extremely tenuous and it often
happens that discussion and debate
in these bodies tends to be based
on narrow local considerations
and not infrequently influenced
by caste and other such considerations. It sometimes happens that
syndicates are heavily loaded
with persons who represent the
government and may be politically
motivated. Circumstances vary
from university to university
also from time to time. But the
administration of the university
is under compulsion of various
kinds and sometimes the real purpose
of a university, vis; the pursuit
of learning at a high level by
a selected body of the most talented
young people in the country, is
obscured and made difficult of
attainment.^{73}

Haggerty points out:

Composed of 100 or more representatives of both academic and
lay interests, the court may have
among its members not only university officers and teachers,
but also alumni, community leaders,
government officials, principals
of related colleges, representatives
of industry and trade, and persons
helping to support the university.
The committee on "Model Act" states
that lay representatives "can
render great service to the university
by their greater knowledge of
the world and their ability to
represent the general desires
and aspirations of society."

77

The court deals with major policy
matters including budget policy
and acts as a consultative body
on any major problem. Its chairman is almost always the Vice-
Chancellor. In some institutions
the court must approve the policies and decisions of the executive and academic councils
but the committee on "Model Act"
is of the opinion that the court
should not be considered a superior
body, and that all three governing
bodies should independently exercise the powers given them by
the legislative act establishing
the university.[74]

Radhakrishnan's Report of the University Education
Commission recommended that the total number of representatives may need to be a little larger than in
unitary and federative universities and suggested
a maximum of 120. There should be a two-fold kind
of balance: (1) between academic and non-academic
members, (2) between university representatives, affiliated colleges representatives and external members.

A third of the university representatives should
be members of constituent colleges. Assuming a university with 20 affiliated colleges and a senate of maximum
size (120), there should be 40 members of the university
staff, 40 representing the affiliated colleges, including
the principal of each college and representatives
of the governing body of each college, and 40 external
members contributed as follows: (a) the alumni associations should elect from among their own members not
more than 10; (b) the donors should elect from among
their own members not more than 5; (c) representatives
of profession, industry and commerce, 10; (d) public
officials as under unitary universities, approximate
total from these sources, 3; (e) nominees of the
Chancellor not more than 6; and (f) the senate itself
should have power to co-opt additonal members up to
6 making a total of 40.[75]

The Executive Council (Syndicate)

The syndicate or the Executive council is the
executive as well as the academic body of the university.

It holds, controls, and administers the property and funds of the university. It formulates the statutes and regulations and has a powerful voice in the administration of the university.

>Although composed of only 15 to 20 members, the executive council may include the same groups of persons, academic and lay, included in the much larger court and also persons nominated by the court. The executive council, almost always presided over by the Vice-Chancellor, administers examinations and raises funds. In some institutions the university court must approve its policies and decisions.[76]

The executive council is the pivotal body in the administration of Indian universities. Since it is bound to wield considerable power, the right choice of members is very important. The University Education Commission also pointed out the importance of the size of the executive council and recommended that it should not be less than 15, nor more than 20 in total membership.

The approximate pattern of the executive council as recommended by the Commission is as follows:[77]

Vice-Chancellor (ex-officio)   1

Treasurer (ex-officio)   1

Deans of Faculties (ex-officio)   1

(If there are more than 8 faculties the deans of the smaller faculties should hold seats on the executive council by rotation. If there are less than 8 faculties, professors who are heads of departments should be elected by the academic council to bring the total up to 8.)

One member of the staff with special
responsibility for residential life   1

(In some universities there is a single person with
chief responsibility for residence; in others such
chief responsibility is shared. In the latter case
those sharing the responsibility should hold this
seat on the executive by rotation.)

Persons elected by the senate from their
number. (University employees will not
be eligible for election in this category.)   4

One person nominated by the High Court of
the Province or State, not necessarily from
their own number.   1

One person nominated by the Public Service
Commission of the Province or State not
necessarily from their own number.   1

Three persons nominated by the Chancellor   3

                                   Total: 20

     All except the ex-officio members of the executive
members of the executive council hold office for three
years. As far as possible, their retirement is staggered
so as to insure a measure of continuity from year
to year in the executive as a whole. The elected
member should be eligible to hold office for two periods,
but thereafter should not be eligible except after
an interval of at least one year.

     Thus, the syndicate is perhaps the most important
body in a university. It consists of vice-chancellors,
treasurer, deans of faculties, elected representatives
of the senate, the faculties and principals. The
academic and non-academic groups are usually evenly
balanced in the syndicate.

The Academic Council

     The academic council of the university is concerned
with academic affairs only. It coordinates the work
of the various faculties and advises the syndicate
on all matters concerning the course of study, curriculums, examinations and degrees. Haggerty gives the
following description:

          Varying in size with the number
          of academic departments and with

the size and complexity of the
academic staff, the academic council includes deans, department
heads, college principals, teachers
chosen by election or seniority,
and sometimes persons with expert
knowledge from outside the university. Almost always presided
over by the Vice-Chancellor, the
academic council has responsibility
for the entire education program,
determining admission requirements,
curriculums, courses of study,
examinations, and degrees; and
therefore also has responsibility
for the university's academic
standards.[79]

The Radhakrishnan University Education Commission
stated that the academic council has at least two
functions of great value and importance.

1.   It is the only body that can coordinate
     between the faculties, and there is a growing
     trend towards courses at the undergraduate
     level in which more than one faculty will
     be concerned.

2.   There should be a two-way traffic of ideas
     and information between the executive and
     the academic councils.

The council should be wholly academic in its
membership and it should not exceed 40 in size. Though
this limit may be pressed hard on one or two of the
larger universities, it is better to keep to this
number even if it means rotation of seats among those
who at smaller universities would all be ex-officio
members. Except where it would cause the limits to
be exceeded, the council comprises: (a) all heads
of departments; (b) ten per cent of the seats on the
council to be filled by teachers other than heads
of departments, elected from their own number; (c)
not more than four members co-opted by reason of their
specialized knowledge.

Elected and co-opted members hold office for
three years, and their retirement is staggered. Elected

members are eligible to hold office for two periods but thereafter are not eligible except after an interval of at least one year.[80]

The Faculties

The faculties of the various schools of the universities are comprised of teachers, heads of the university departments, and principals of the colleges affiliated with the universities. They deal with the academic matters, such as the framing of courses, the organization of teaching and supervision of examinations, together with the academic council. Each faculty, the Commission recommended, should comprise: (a) the professors and readers in the subjects assigned to that faculty by the academic council; (b) not more than half the number consisting of other teachers of the faculty subjects. These should be appointed to membership of the faculty by the academic council on the recommendation of the faculty. They should not be eligible except after an interval of at least one year; and (c) not more than three persons co-opted by reason of their specialized knowledge.

The Commission also pointed out that the deans of the faculties should be elected by the professors in each faculty who are heads of the departments, from among their own number. The dean should hold office for two years and should be eligible for re-election for a second term of two years. Thereafter he should not be eligible for re-election if there are other professors who are heads of departments in the faculty who have not served as deans.[81]

The number of faculties in each university is prescribed by its statutes. Headed by a dean, each faculty usually consists of several teachers from each department within its field of study and sometimes a few persons with expert knowledge from outside the university. Of the members from the university in each faculty, some must be department heads and not more than one may come from each faculty has charge of the courses of study and directs

the research work in its respective departments.[82]

The Board of Studies

The boards of studies are usually composed of
university teachers, senior teachers from related
colleges, and often teachers from other universities.
Usually, the head of the department is ex-officio
chairman of its board. Generally, subject to the approval
of the academic council and sometimes of the executive
council, the boards prepare courses of study, recommend
textbooks, and suggest persons to act as examiners.[83]

The Radhakrishnan Report emphasized the importance
of having a board of studies for each department:

> There should be a board of studies
> for each department. It should
> be an internal body but with power
> to co-opt one member, from outside
> the university. The head of the
> department should be the chairman
> of the board, which should comprise
> the professors and readers in
> the department and all full-time
> members of teaching staff of five
> years' standing. Members of cognate
> or related departments may be
> invited to attend meetings of
> the board, though not as members
> of it. In small departments it
> is desirable that this should
> be done.[84]

The university has, thus, a board of studies
for every subject or group of subjects. As it has
already been noted, the board recommends courses of
study, textbooks, examiners, examinations, and reports
of any matter referred to it by the faculties. Some
universities have other internal officers for their
administration, such as selection committees, board
of post-graduate studies and/or research, board of
inspection and board of university teaching.

The university faculty should be allotted more
power and responsibility in the conduct of university

affairs; the teachers also should have adequate representation in the executive council and the court. Besides, one or two student representatives could be added to the list, though it is a controversial issue among the Indian educators. The academic council, which deals with the academic affairs of the university, also could benefit from student delegation.

FOOTNOTES

[1] Association of Indian Universities, Universities Handbook of India 1981-82 (New Delhi: Raja Printers, 1981), p. v.

[2] Ministry of Education, Educational Activities of the Government of India (Delhi-6: Government of India Press, 1963), pp. 90-91.

[3] Ibid., pp. 93-94.

[4] Ibid., pp. 92-93.

[5] Ibid., pp. 91-92.

[6] Ibid.

[7] Ministry of Education, Government of India, Report 1967-68, p. 1.

[8] Ibid.

[9] Ibid., pp. 265-66.

[10] Ibid., p. 267.

[11] Haggerty, Higher and Professional Education in India, p. 25.

[12] J. B. Naik, The Role of Government in Indian Education (Delhi: National Council of Educational Research and Training, Ministry of Education, 1962), pp. 1-17.

[13] Margert Cormack, She Who Rides a Peacock (Bombay: Asia Publishing House, 1961), p. 33.

[14] Sir John Sargent, Society Schools and Progress In India (Oxford, London, New York: Pergamon Press, 1968), p. 92.

[15] Siqueira, op.cit., p. 251.

[16] National Council of Educational Research Training, The Indian Year Book of Education 1961 (New Delhi: Sree Saraswathy Press Ltd., 1965) p. 24.

[17] The Report of the University Education Commission 1948-1949, pp. 2-3.

[18]Ibid., pp. 115-116.

[19]Inter-University Board of India and Ceylon "University News," February-March 1964, p. 1.

[20]Report of the Education Commission, 1964-66, p. 613.

[21]Ibid., pp. 274-75.

[22]Ibid., p. 276.

[23]The Report of the Education Commission, 1964-66, p. 67.

[24]Ibid., p. 68.

[25]Ibid., p. 1.

[26]Ibid., p. 65.

[27]Ibid.

[28]The Report of the University Grants Commission, 1953-1957, p. 1.

[29]Ibid., p. 6.

[30]Ibid., p. 8.

[31]Ibid., pp. 6-7

[32]University Grants Commission, Handbook of Universities in India, pp. 14-15.

[33]Ibid., p. 15.

[34]"Chronicle of Higher Education and Research in India," University News, VIII (June, 1970), 151.

[35]Shri Surag Bhan, op. cit., p. 18.

[36]Report of the University Grants Commission, 1953-57, pp. 8-9.

[37]India: A Reference Annual, 1969, p. 69.

[38]Planning Commission, First Five-Year Plan, 1951-56 (Delhi: Government of India, 1952), p. 525.

[39] Planning Commission, Second Five-Year Plan, 1956-61, A Draft Outline (Delhi: Government of India, 1956), p. 183.

[40] Government of India Planning Commission, The New India (New York: The Macmillan Company, 1958), p. 337.

[41] Ibid.

[42] Lakshmanaswami Mudaliar, Education in India (Bombay: Asia Publishing House, 1960), p. 338.

[43] Facts About India, p. 148.

[44] Planning Commission, Third-Five Year Plan, 1961-66 (Delhi: Government of India, 1961), p. 573.

[45] India: A Reference Annual, 1969, p. 212.

[46] Ministry of Education, Government of India, Report 1966-67, p. 2.

[47] India News, IX (May 29, 1970), 1.

[48] India News, IX (April 24, 1970), 3.

[49] Ministry of Information and Broadcasting Government of India, India A Reference Annual, 1980 (New Delhi: Government of India Press, 1980), p. 46.

[50] Ibid.

[51] Education in Eighteen Years of Freedom, pp. 11-12.

[52] Haggerty, op. cit., pp. 26-27.

[53] Ibid., p. 27.

[54] The Report of the University Education Commission 1948-9, p. 18.

[55] D. D. Tewari, "Decentralization in Education," Indian Education: Journal of the All-India Federation of Educational Associations, VII (March, 1960), pp. 4-19.

[56] Report of the Education Commission, 1964-66, p. 74.

[57] Report of the Committee Members of Parliament on Education, 1967, pp. 18-19.

87

[58]University Grants Commission Report, 1966-67, p. 56.

[59]A Yearbook of the Commonwealth (London: Her Majesty's Stationery Office, 1969), p. 1537.

[60]Ibid.

[61]Ibid.

[62]Report of the University Education Commission, 1948-49, p. 421.

[63]World Survey of Education, p. 607.

[64]The Report of the University Education Commission, 1948-49, p. 421.

[65]Ibid., pp. 421-22.

[66]Ibid., p. 422

[67]Ibid., p. 423.

[68]Ibid., p. 424.

[69]Haggerty, op. cit., p. 82.

[70]The Report of the University Education Commission, 1948-49, p. 421.

[71]Haggerty, op. cit., p. 86.

[72]Samuel Mathai, "University Administration," Education Quarterly, (October, 1967), p. 11.

[73]Ibid., p. 12.

[74]Haggerty, op. cit., p. 86.

[75]Report of the University Education Commission, 1948-49, p. 431.

[76]Haggerty, op. cit., p. 86.

[77]The Report of the University Education Commission, 1948-49, p. 426.

[78]Ibid., pp. 426-27.

[79]Haggerty, op. cit., p. 86.

[80]Report of the University Education Commission, 1948-49,
p. 427.

[81]Ibid., pp. 427-28.

[82]Haggerty, op. cit., p. 87.

[83]Ibid.

[84]The Report of the University Education Commission, 1948-
49, p. 428.

CHAPTER IV

HIGHER EDUCATIONAL PROGRAMME

The post-secondary education in India is mainly
imparted through: (1) pre-university, (2) arts and
science colleges, (3) professional and special education
colleges, (4) universities, and (5) research institutions.
The 1956 University Grants Commission Act points out:

> Besides universities, there are
> a large number of institutions
> which impart higher learning.
> The Birla Institute of Technology
> and Science, Pilani, the India
> Agricultural Research Institute,
> New Delhi, the Indian Institute
> of Science, Bangalore, the Jamia
> Millia Islamia, New Delhi, the
> Indian School of International
> Studies, New Delhi, the Gurukul
> Kangri Vishwavidyalays, Hardwar,
> the Kashi Vidyapith, Varanasi,
> Gujarat Vidyapith, Ahamedabad,
> Tata Institute of Social Science,
> Bombay and the Indian School of
> Mines, Dhanbad, are all deemed
> to be universities for the purposes
> of University Grants Commission
> Act, 1956. . . .[1]

Pre-University Educational Programme

At present the pre-university programme is a post-
secondary education designed for two years; and preceding
admission into the three year degree programme in
the universities or in the colleges. The students
are required to pass the pre-university examination
before being admitted into the three-year degree courses.
It is a new educational programme started in accordance
with the recommendation of the Education Commissions
and University Grants Commission. Until recently
the duration of the academic course at the pre-university level was only one year in most of the states.
But the 1966 Report of the Education Commission recommended:

> The duration of the academic course
> at the higher secondary state

(or the pre-university) stage
should be uniformly raised to
two years in all parts of the
country under phased plan. The
curriculum should include two
languages, three subjects selected
from a prescribed list of work-
experience and social service,
physical and health education,
and education in moral and social
values. The academic control
of this stage should be entrusted
to a single authority in each
State on which the universities
should have adequate representation.[2]

Three-Year Degree Course

The three-year degree course is designed for the
students who have satisfactorily completed their studies
in the pre-university programme, and passed pre-university public examination, conducted by the university.
At the end of the three-year degree course, each student
has to sit for the external final examination set
by the same university in his jurisdiction in order
to get a bachelor's degree in arts and science.

The Ministry of Education describes how the three-
year degree course has been introduced in the Indian
universities:

A very significant development
in university education in the
post Independence period has been
the institution of the three-year
degree course. The University
Education Commission and the Secondary Education Commission had
both recommended a reorganization
of the national system of education.
The recommendations of the Secondary
Education Commission were considered
by the Conference of Vice-Chancellors convened in 1955. The
Central Advisory Board of Education considered the matter at
its meeting held in 1956 and recommended a national pattern of

education which the first eight
years of integrated elementary
(basic education are to be followed by three years of higher
secondary education are to be
latter by three years of university education leading to the
first degree. The three-year
degree course thus became a part
of an over-all scheme to improve
the quality of university and
secondary education. A committee
was set up in October 1956, under
the chairmanship of Dr. C. D.
Deshmukh, to work out the esti-
mates to expenditure involved
in introducing this important
reform. It was recommended that
the course should be introduced
in as many universities as possible
during the Second Plan itself.[3]

The University Grants Commission has been closely
associated with the proposal made by the Government
of India for the introduction of a three-year degree
course in Indian universities. The University Grants
Commission estimated the total amount of money which
would be required to maintain the three-year degree
plan for four years would be about Rs. 25 crores.
This cost was to be shared between the Central and
State Governments in equal proportion. The Central
Government had to provide 7-1/2 crores in the first
stage. An equal amount was paid by the State Government,
including contributions from private management. Thus
the total amount provided was 15 crores of rupees
which was sufficient for upgrading some 180 existing
intermediate colleges and re-organizing some 360 degree
colleges. This was taken as a target for the second
five-year plan (1956-1961).[4]

In order to facilitate the introduction of the
three-year degree course, the University Grants Commission assisted 42 universities and 733 colleges
affiliated to them by providing additional staff,
classroom accommodations, library and laboratory
facilities. The grants which were made available
by the Commission were intended to help the institutions concerned to provide essential academic and

physical facilities for the three-year degree course, and thereby to bring about an improvement in the quality and standards of undergraduate education. Recurring grants were provided for four years starting from the year in which the three year degree course was introduced. Non-recurring grants admissible under the scheme had to be utilized by March 31, 1966. During 1966-67 grants amounting to Rs. 94 lakhs for the admissible recurring and non-recurring expenditure were released to the universities and colleges.[5]

The three-year degree course is part of an overall scheme to improve the quality of college and secondary education in India. The degree course was introduced with the hope that it would provide an opportunity to revise the syllabi, introduce general education courses, reduce overcrowding in colleges, improve the teacher-pupil ratio, strengthen laboratories, replenish libraries and, wherever possible, institute a sound tutorial system.[6] At present, almost all the universities in India have the three-year degree programme.

The main idea in planning this new scheme was to alter the former pattern of university education by replacing the four years of the old degree course with two years of pre-university and a three-year degree course.

As has been pointed out already, no student is admitted to the three-year degree course of any college unless he has passed satisfactorily the pre-university examination conducted by the universities. The promotion for higher studies depends upon the results of the pre-university examination. Again in the final or third year of the degree course, the student is examined by the university. Generally, the public examination conducted by the university covers the entire course work studied for the three years, and is the same for all the affiliated colleges of the university. The students who pass this examination are granted degrees by the university and not by their colleges. Hence, the degree is not dependent upon the standards of a college as it is in the United States.

Regarding the three-year degree (first degree course) for arts and science, the University Education Commission recommended the following:

() The Federal language, or if that happens to be the mother tongue, a Classical or Modern Indian Language; (2) English.

For arts students not less than two special subjects, preferably one from each group: (1) Humanities and Social Studies, (2) A Classical or a Modern Indian Language, (3) English, French or German, (4) Philosophy, (5) History, (6) Mathematics, (7) Fine Arts, (8) Politics, (9) Economics, (10) Sociology, (11) Psychology, (12) Anthropology, (13) Geography, (14) Home Economics.

For science students, not less than two special subjects from the following list:

(1) Mathematics, (2) Physics, (3) Chemistry, (4) Botany, (5) Zoology, (6) Geology.

In summary, the abolition of the intermediate stage of the university education and the introduction of a three-year degree course is a significant development in university education in Indian's post-Independence period; this is a clear indication that higher education in India has been reorganized. This three-year degree course thus became a part of an overall scheme to improve the quality of university education. Though the basic character of education has not changed much after the introduction of the three-year degree course, there were a few changes in the courses of the arts and science degree programme and the introduction of regional media of instruction. There is an urgent need to revise the curriculum and introduce new courses according to the needs of each college and university.

By this scheme of three-year degree courses, the students are more prepared for taking up the graduate studies since they are exposed to more courses of study. Moreover, an additional year would prevent the students from entering in the graduate school before they are mature enough to pursue higher studies.

Graduate, Post-Graduate Studies and Research

As noted earlier, five academic years are required to complete a bachelor's degree in arts and science-- two years for pre-university and three years for three-year degree courses. So a regular student would

95

take his bachelor's degree after fifteen years of school and college studies. "The Master's degree will be taken in the case of the honours candidate one year, and in the case of the pass candidate two years, after he takes his Bachelor's degree."[8]

Table 2 shows the number of years of schooling time for a regular student for taking qualifying and degree examinations in comparison with England and America. The educational pattern of India (1966) is given in Figure 3.

The term "post-graduate training" in India is applied to the training of students after the M.A. degrees. It includes advanced study of one special subject of an extensive and intensive nature. It can only be undertaken by capable students under guidance of qualified teachers.

The post-graduate classes are intended: (1) to train teachers for all levels of higher education, (2) to train experts for many services in the non-academic fields, such as government, industry, commerce, agriculture and public welfare, and (3) to train research personnel.[9]

Further, the University Education Commission has recommended:

1. That students be admitted to colleges and universities in the faculties of arts and science, and to such professional schools as do not require more advanced preparation, after successful completion of twelve years of schooling or its equivalent; that is after they have passed the qualifying test which will correspond to the present intermediate standard;

2. That the Master's degree be given to honours students after one year of study beyond the bachelor's degree;

3. That both universities and secondary schools begin study of the theory and practice of general education, and undertake preparation of syllabi and reading matter somewhat after the manner outlined in this section; that

studies be made by individuals and by educational groups in various fields; and that literature for general education courses be developed which will give the student the best of thinking and working in each field, and with the relations of related fields--this without requiring more than a fair share of the student's time;

4. That without unnecessary delay the principles and practice of general education be introduced, so as to correct the extreme specialization which now is common is our intermediate and degree programmes;

5. That the relations of general and special education be worked out for each field, keeping in mind the general interests of the student as a personality and a citizen, and his special occupational interest.[10]

An urgent need in the field of higher education in India since Independence has been the strengthening of post-graduate teaching and research. This has been realized by the leaders of India from the beginning of independence. The importance of post-graduate training and research was stressed by the University Education Commission:

Human civilization has derived
great benefits from the efforts
of specialists who have penetrated
ever more deeply into the secrets
of nature and the motives and
processes of human behavior,
individual and social. To a constantly increasing extent, modern
life is the outcome of research.
To quote Whitehead, "a progressive
society depends on its inclusion
of three groups: scholars, discoverers, inventors." While the
scholars rediscover the past and
set before us ideals of wisdom,
beauty and goodness, discoverers
find out new truths, and inventors
apply them to present needs.
The universities are the chief

TABLE 2

NORMAL NUMBER OF YEARS OF SCHOOLING

(Comparison with U.S.A. and England)

Country	High School or Matric	Inter or Pre-University (Junior College)	Bachelor's Degree	Master's Degree	Doctorate
India	10	12	15	16 (for honours) 17 (for pass)	18
England	11	13	16	17	18
U.S.A.	12	14	16	17	19

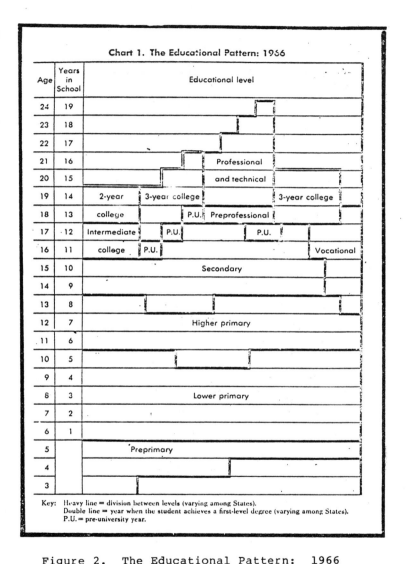

Chart 1. The Educational Pattern: 1966

Age	Years in School	Educational level
24	19	
23	18	
22	17	
21	16	Professional
20	15	and technical
19	14	2-year 3-year college 3-year college
18	13	college P.U. Preprofessional
17	12	Intermediate P.U. P.U.
16	11	college P.U. Vocational
15	10	Secondary
14	9	
13	8	
12	7	Higher primary
11	6	
10	5	
9	4	
8	3	Lower primary
7	2	
6	1	
5		Preprimary
4		
3		

Key: Heavy line = division between levels (varying among States).
Double line = year when the student achieves a first-level degree (varying among States).
P.U. = pre-university year.

Figure 2. The Educational Pattern: 1966

Taken from **Higher and Professional Education in India**,
p. 18.

agencies for producing these types
of men who will fuse progressive
activities into an effective instrument. Universities are responsible
for extending boundaries of knowledge as for the training of citizens:
in fact, the advancement of knowledge is a necessary condition
of the continued vitality of their
teaching, for unless a study is
rooted in research, it will die.
. . . Advancement of knowledge
is a duty primarily of teachers
and it is for them to inspire
their students with a spirit of
inquiry by their own contributions
to knowledge.[11]

About the post-graduate degree, the Commission
stated:

We, therefore, recommend that
there should be a certain uniformity
in the regulations for the M.A.
and M.Sc. degrees in all the
universities. A pass graduate
should study for at least two
years and an honours graduate
at least one year for these degrees. Teaching should be properly organized by means of regular
lectures, seminars and library
work for the arts students, and
by the same course along with
laboratory work for the science
students; it should include advanced training and the latest
methods of research in the special
subject of study so as to equip
the student to be able to carry
on independent investigations,
but it should not include actual
research. A candidate for M.A.
or M.Sc. degree should show a
high degree of scholarship and
achievement in his examination,
which should be conducted by papers
and a <u>viva voce test</u>, to be sup-

100

plemented by a practical examination in science subjects.[12]

It also has been recommended that a great care
should be taken with regard to the admission of students
to the M.A. or M.Sc. classes. The whole of the students'
grades or transcript should be scrutinized from the
high school to the B.A. and B.Sc. There should not
be any type of provincial restrictions. The Government
of India should make it a condition that no university
should receive a government grant unless it sets admissions standards on the basis of merit alone and on
an all India basis. "Emphasis should be placed on
the capacity and quality of students and not on their
number. These classes should be characterized by
their small numbers and by the closest personal touch
with senior staff directing their studies.[13] Only
a successful researcher in his subject was to teach
these classes.

Although post-graduate training and research
in the universities have made considerable progress
during the past twenty-three years, the quality and
quantity of research declined.

The Commission comments on this unfortunate
situation and its causes:

> Unfortunately there are signs
> of the steady decline in the qual-
> ity and quantity of research at
> our universities. There are several
> causes, but the most important
> is that most of the leaders of
> research in different fields have
> either left the universities or
> are on the verge of retirement
> and the universities have not
> been able to find suitable suc-
> cessors to continue the research
> tradition initiated and fostered
> by these pioneers. Ever since
> the higher administrative services
> were thrown open to Indian gradu-
> ates the universities have had
> to compete with the Government,
> which is the largest employer
> in India, for recruitment of their

teaching staff. The universities
could not attract the best men
to their staff and during the
last ten years a number of brilliant teachers have left the universities for government service,
as they were offered better salaries
and prospects there.[14]

The universities were directed by the University
Education Commission to attract capable students to
take up the teaching profession in colleges and universities. This was to be done by providing decent salaries
and other benefits, on an all-India basis to improve
the teaching, learning, and research work in the Indian
colleges and universities.

The 1964-66 Report of the University Education
Commission pointed out the urgent need of taking necessary measures to improve teaching and research work
in the institutions of higher learning. The report
urged that: (1) A documentation centre and a national
clearing house in educational research should be developed at the NCERT. (2) Educational research has to
be developed in teams and in inter-disciplinary fields.
Although all training colleges should do some research,
the restriction of educational research work to training
colleges has hampered its growth. It will be the
special responsibility of School of Education to develop
educational research largely in collaboration with
other departments. (3) It is desirable to set up
a National Academy of Education consisting of eminent
educationists, similar to the National Institute of
Science, to promote educational thought and research.
This should be essentially a non-official professional
body. But it should receive adequate financial support
from the Government of India. (4) An Education Research Council should be set up in the Ministry of
Education for the promotion of research. (5) There
is urgent need to provide good specialized training
for research work and service for data processing,
statistical analysis and consultation. (6) It would
be the responsibility of the NCERT at the national
level and the state Institutes of Education at the
state level to bridge the serious gap between the
educational research and current school practices.
A similar role will have to be played by the UGC in
the field of higher education. (7) The total expendi-

ture on education research has to be increased considerably, the goal being to devote about one percent
of the state expenditure on education to it.[15]

To promote post-graduate teaching and research,
the University Grants Commission has attempted to
develop some centres of advance studies and research.
The Commission, in consultation with the universities,
has undertaken a scheme for developing a limited number
of university departments for advanced training and
research in certain selected fields. The purpose
of the scheme is to encourage the pursuit of "excellence"
and team work in studies and research and to accelerate
the realization of "international standards" in special
fields. With this object in view it is proposed to
give active support and substantial assistance to
promising departments in the universities carefully
selected on the following basis: quality and extent
of work already done by them; their reputation and
contribution to research; and their potentiality for
further development.[16]

The University Grants Commission also suggested
that it would be desirable to establish post-graduate
centre as a preparatory step for the establishment
of new universities. Such centres could be organized
by the local colleges and the universities with which
they were affiliated, on cooperative basis. The opinion
of the Commission was that the centres of post-graduate
studies need not necessarily be converted into universities, but it would be desirable to have a well-developed centre for post-graduate studies, before a new
university is established. The minimum requirements
of staff, library, and laboratory and other facilities
which would be needed by a centre of post-graduate
studies were also examined.[17]

Many colleges and universities have started post-
graduate courses. For instance, in 1966-67, 447 affiliated colleges were conducting post-graduate studies
and research. A significant amount of financial assistance has been given by the Commission for the development of post-graduate studies in science subjects
and the humanities and social sciences on a sharing
basis.

The amount granted during the fourth five-year
plan is given below:

For the development of post-graduate
studies in the humanities and
social sciences, assistance from
the Commission to a college during
the Fourth Plan period (inclusive
of payments in respect of continuing projects from the earlier
Plan periods) is limited to Rs.
1,00000. For post-graduate departments in science subjects,
the Commission's grant to a college is limited to Rs. 1,0000
each for physics and chemistry,
Rs. 75,000 each for botany, zoology, geology, home science and
biochemistry, and Rs. 50,000 each
for anthropology, geography and
mathematics (including statistics). The Commission's assistance is limited to 50% of the
approved cost of buildings and
expenditure on additional teaching
staff, and 75% for equipment and
books. The prescribed matching
share has to be contributed by
the college and the Commission
does not share expenditure on
contingencies, and non-teaching
staff. An assurance is required
that additional posts created
under the scheme will be continued
and maintained by the college
concerned when assistance from
the Commission for this purpose
ceases. During the Third Plan,
the Commission approved the development of facilities for post-
graduate education in science
subjects in 85 affiliated colleges
and sanctioned grants amounting
to Rs. 1.05 crores. Grants amounting
to Rs. 47.37 lakhs were also approved for 71 colleges for the
development of post-graduate studies
in science subjects and the humanities including social science
during 1966-67 amounted
to Rs. 7.46 lakhs and Rs. 8.17 Lakhs,
respectively.[18]

A special directive of the University Grants Commission is that "Universities should join together, at the regional and national levels, in cooperative programmes and supplement mutually their available facilities, especially in research."[19]

As in other spheres of socio-economic endeavor, independence provided an unlimited freedom for research development. There are three main organizations, namely, the National Council for Educational Research and Training, the Council of Scientific and Industrial Research, and the Atomic Energy Department which are engaged in research activities.

In 1961 the National Council for Educational Research and Training was set up as an autonomous organization with the responsibility of providing national leadership in educational research and training. Educational research in India had 'til recently been a neglected area. A vast amount required to be done to make up the leeway. No single organization could hope to do this effectively. The Council has, therefore, sought to emphasize the cooperative aspect of research work by involving a number of institutions and organizations in its programmes.

In the choice of problems and projects, the need to make research functional and to relate its findings to the needs of the educational system is a top priority. Research problems of national importance in various fields, are located and arranged in order of priority relative to the requirements of State departments of education, training colleges, universities and other educational institutions. The Council also organizes research evaluation studies, utilizing the available resources. It is

preparing a carefully designed
blue-print of important educational problems facing country
today and in the immediate future
at all levels of the educational
system. To achieve a high standard of research work, the Council
maintains close touch with research developments in other countries, and in other parallel
fields within the country.[20]

Besides the research programmes, the council has
grant-in-aid schemes under which financial assistance
is given to outside agencies such as colleges, university education departments and research institutions
to enable them to undertake research into educational
problems and also to publish outstanding research
work.[21]

Also the laboratories of the Council provide
facilities for training of research workers for award
of higher degrees. Many of these laboratories and
institutes are recognized by the universities as centres
for advanced research leading to Ph.D. degree. Some
of the laboratories also provide short and long-term
training course, higher training courses and summer
schools from time to time. The council awards a large
number of senior and junior research fellowships to
the universities and research institutes for brilliant
younger scientists to encourage research as a career.
"In addition to their own research programmes, the
National Laboratories undertake research projects spon-
sored by the industry and other users' organizations.
During 1964, 180 research schemes were taken up at 18
laboratories. Work on 57 schemes was completed and results were made available to the concerned parties."[22]

To summarize, an urgent need since Independence
has been the strengthening of the post-graduate studies
and research. This has been realized by the educational
and national leaders of India from the beginning of
independence. Since teaching and advancement of knowledge is the primary function of the universities and
colleges, the graduate studies should be strengthened
by introducting more independent studies, and research
in the specialized field of studies at the master's
level. At the Ph.D. level one or two years of regular

course work could be offered in the specialized field of study, as it is done in the United States and elsewhere, in addition to the dissertation. The pursuit of excellence should be to meet the international standards in the field of specialization.

As the 1948-49 University Education Commission has pointed out, there was a steady decline in the quality and quantity of research for a time because of a number of leaders of research had left for Government service as they were offered better salaries. Later on several measures were taken to improve teaching and research work in the institutions of higher learning. The establishment of research centres, research organizations, and grant-in-aid schemes, and cooperative research programmes have provided a greater scope for research development. As has been pointed out, at present there is hardly any subject in which India is not engaged in the acquisition and pursuit of knowledge. This is accomplished through: National Council for Educational Research and Training, the Council of Scientific and Industrial Research and the Atomic Energy Department. This is only the beginning stage of research development. More emphasis on quality is needed.

Technical and Scientific Education

Another significant area of progress in the field of higher education is the development of Technical Education in India since Independence. The technical and scientific education have expanded considerably during this period of 23 years. (See Figure 4.) In 1947, the country was faced with the great challenge of developing a predominantly agricultural economy into a major industrial economy. Regarding it the Ministry of Education stated thus:

> Perhaps one of the most remarkable achievements in India during the last 18 years of independence is the phenomenal growth of technical education. Almost from scratch the country had to build up its technical education within a very short period.

> In 1947, India produced only 930 graduates in engineering and 320

107

graduates in technology. Facilities for advanced training and research at post-graduate level in technology were very meagre and in engineering almost nil. The growth of technical education during the last 18 years is reflected, both in the rapid increases in the student enrollment and the number of institutions. As against an annual admission of 3,000 students for the first degree courses and 3,700 students for diploma courses in 1947, the admission capacity in technical institutions for first degree was 23,760 and that of diploma 46,250. Against only 38 institutions for first degree and 53 for diploma in 1947, in 1964-65 the number of degree institutions has gone up to 131 and that of diploma to 264.[23]

At present, there are many technical schools such as agriculture, engineering, forestry, industry, medicine, etc. Enrollment in such institutions in 1950 was about 266,000, as against only 2,336 in 1947. The number of students enrolled was 187,000. Now it is about 3 million. Starting almost from scratch, there are now approximately 140 engineering and technical institutions which award graduate or post-graduate degrees. The admission capacity in engineering and technology institutions now is 25,000 at the degree level and 48,600 at the diploma level. This is indicative of the vast educational expansion the Government of India consciously encouraged and brought about since independence.[24]

Regarding the expansion of the technical education, the following facts are given:

In 1967-68 about 13,900 persons came out with degrees in engineering and technology. There were 284 technical institutions for diploma courses with facilities for admitting some 48,000 students every year. In 1967-68, about 21,000 persons received diplomas.

The number of medical colleges (of all categories) and veterinary colleges in 1965-66 was 181, they admitted annually about 61,000 students. About a sixth of the students attending colleges get scholarships or stipends.[25]

With the view to improving the quality and quantity of different classes of engineers and technologists, the University Education Commission has recommended the following:

1. That the existing engineering and technological institutes of the country, whatever be their origin or method of administration should be regarded as national assets, and steps should be taken to improve their usefulness according to the recommendations of the Advisory Panel of Engineers and Technologists to be set up;

2. the number of engineering schools of different grades be increased particularly for training of grades 4 and 5 (foremet craftsmen, draftsmen, overseers, etc.);

3. that engineering schools cover a larger number of fields and branches of engineering to meet the increasingly varied needs of the country. If there is unemployment among competent engineers it is because too many are trained in some phases of engineering and too few in others;

4. that engineering courses of study include general education and basic physical and engineering sciences, probably fewer applied courses, and toward the end of the course specialisation in some specific field. The first years or more of each course should in general be common to all branches of engineering;

5. that, as effective engineering education requires works practice along with academic

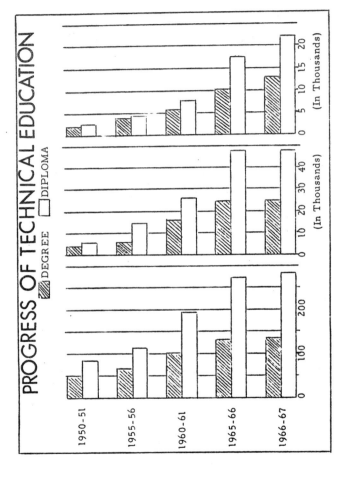

Figure 3. Progress of Technical Education

Taken from: Education in India, A Graphic Presentation. India Ministry of Education.

110

study, this be secured as work during vacations or as post-graduate works training, or as participation in work and study programme during the under graduate years;

6. That wherever possible the existing engineering and technological colleges be upgraded for post-graduate training and research in selected subjects. This requires a class of teachers with different upbringing, habits, and service conditions than the present staffs; hence it may not always be possible to upgrade the present institutes;

7. that steps be taken to start without delay the higher technological institutes as recommended by the Higher Technological Education Committee, for training much needed engineer-scientists and design and development engineers;

8. that inquiries be made of possibilities for training for graduate engineers and engineer scientists as employees in American industries and other institutions, so that practical "know how" may be quickly secured for India's industries;

9. that in establishing new engineering colleges or institutes, there be fresh, critical inquiry as to the types of engineering service needed in India. Uncritical repetition and imitation of existing institutions here and abroad should be avoided. Especially consideration should be given to training which will prepare students to become competent and self-reliant, who will have the initiative and courage to start new industries, even if on a very small scale, to the end that there shall be many sources of initiative and responsibility in India, and that a top-heavy economic bureaucracy may not be necessary;

10. that engineering colleges be not controlled or dominated in their administration by ministries or other government departments. They should be closely associated with

universities, and appointments should be
made in the manner indicated elsewhere in
this report; or if made by the engineering department or college, with the approval
and active participation of the university
administration, where the relationship makes
that desirable;

11. that Faculties of Engineering be called
"Faculties of Engineering and Technology"
and should include teachers representing
different branches of engineering and technology, a few scientists, teacher of humanities and commerce, and a number of
practicing engineers and technologists;

12. that the proposed Central Universities Grants
Commission be helped by a Standing Advisory
Panel for Engineering and Technology, as
the fulfilment of the programme of Engineering and Technology, as the fulfilment
of the programme of Engineering and Technical Education, as visualized by us, will
require large grants from the Centre.[26]

For the development of technical and scientific
education in India, All-India Council for Technical
Education was constituted. The ministry of education
describes its functions as follows:

The All India Council for Technical Education was constituted
in November, 1945. It is composed
of representatives of Union and
State Governments. Parliament
and associations in the fields
of commerce, industry, labour,
the professions and education.
Though the Council has advisory
functions only, experience shows
that its recommendations have
invariably been accepted by the
Union and State Governments.
The four Regional Committees with
their offices at Kanpur, Madras,
Bombay and Calcutta cover a group
of States each and perform approximately the same functions

112

in the development of technical
education in their respective
regions as does the All India
Council for the country as a
whole. The All India Council
for Technical Education has set
up seven Boards of Technical
Studies to advise the Council
on such technical matters as the
preparation of model courses of
studies, laying down standards
and regulating the award of national diplomas. On the recommendation of the All India Council
for Technical Education, each
State has set up a Board of Technical Education.[27]

Another important feature of the post-independence
period is the establishment of Indian Institutes of
Technology at Kanpur, Madras, Bombay and Delhi in col-
laboration with the Governments of United States, West
Germany, USSR and Great Britain respectively on the
pattern of the Indian Institute of Technology, Kharagpur.
These institutes were declared Institutions of National
Importance by an Act of Parliament in 1961. Other
specialised institutions administered by the Union
Ministry of Education are the School of Planning and
Architecture, Delhi; the Indian School of Mines, Dhanbad;
the All India Institutes of Management at Calcutta and
Ahamedabad; and the National Institute of Training in
Industrial Engineering.[28]

This recognition of the importance
of agricultural education led
not only to the expansion facilities but also to a reorganisation
of agricultural education in the
existing as well as new institutions set up to provide facilities for training of agricultural
workers in the various branches
of agricultural sciences with
particular emphasis on the quality
of educational programmes.

In the course of the last eighteen
years the number of agricultural

and veterinary colleges have grown
from 17 and 6 to 67 and 19 respectively. The intake capacity of
the agricultural colleges in undergraduate classes has swelled from
1,500 to 8,900 per annum. Post
graduate training facilities leading
to M.Sc. and Ph.D. degrees are
available for 1300 and 150 students
respectively as compared to less
than a total of 100 in 1947.

. . . With a view to attract meritor-
ious students to agricultural
and veterinary colleges, the Indian
Council of Agricultural Research
instituted in 1963 the award of
250 merit scholarships for undergraduate studies. In addition,
the Council has been extending
the facility for postgraduate
studies. The number of scholarships and fellowships at the post-
graduate level has been raised
to 200 since 1965-66.[29]

There were only 15 medical colleges in the country
with an annual enrollment of 1,200, till 1946. Little
or no emphasis was laid on postgraduate education and
training of specialists even by the oldest colleges in
India. Only a handful of doctors were qualified for
MD and MS in general medicine and surgery. Some of those
who wished to be qualified in various specialities pro-
ceeded abroad for training.

The number of medical colleges
which stood at 30 with an admission
capacity of 2,489 at the beginning
of the First Five-Year Plan increased
in the admission capacity of 3,958.
By the end of the Second Plan,
the number of medical colleges
increased to 66 with an admission
capacity of 6,846. The target
for the Third Plan was 18 more
medical colleges to bring the
total up to 75. This target was
achieved by 1963 and at present

114

there are 81 medical colleges
with an admission capacity of
over 10,000. By the end of the
Third Plan, it is expected that
there will be a total of 85 medical
colleges. The Mudaliar Committee
has recommended that it would
perhaps be a safe target to aim
to have one doctor for over 3,000-
3,500 population at the end of
the Fourth Plan period. There
should be one medical college
for at least 5 million population
which would mean that there should
be 90 medical colleges for the
existing population, and for the
anticipated population in 1971,
the number of medical colleges
will have to be nearer 100.
Similar targets have to be fixed
for dental, nursing, pharmaceu-
tical and other pharamedical.[30]

To study and improve technical education in India,
the Education Ministry has set up a committee chaired
by Mr. Damodaran. Two foreign experts have been invited
to advise the Damodarn Committee on technical education.
The present system of technical education, particularly
at the poly-technic level, has come in for critical
comment from two foreign experts. Mr. G. Ross Henninger
of the U.S. and Mr. B. Houghton of the U.K. - "have expressed the view that besides a mere change in curriculum, a drastic improvement in the methods of teaching
will be necessary to produce competent engineers."[31]

Besides these courses in technical education, the
Indian institutions of higher learning are offering
courses in nursing, pharmacy, dentistry, architecture,
business administration and commerce, forestry, home
science, journalism, law, library science, physical
education, public administration, and social work.

To summarize the phenomenal growth of technical
and scientific education is a remarkable achievement
in India since independence. The number of technical
and scientific institutions have increased in rapid
pace. For example, against only 38 institutions for
first degree and 53 for diploma in 1947, in 1964-65 the

number of degree institutions has shot up to 131 and
that of diploma to 264. The enrollment in technical
education has also increased more than eightfold in 18
years. Professional and technical education of a advanced nature, particularly in the fields of agriculture,
medicine and technology is required for the accomplish-
ment of the goals of India's developmental plans: an
adequate supply of food, health conditions equal to the
best modern medicine can provide, and higher technological and industrial production.

     In a broadcast to the Nation (India) Prime Minister
Mrs. Indira Gandhi, stated:

          In years since independence, the
          nation has many achievements to
          its credit--vast and complex indus-
          trial enterprises, agrarian reforms
          including abolition of zamindari
          system, mass education including
          substantial expansion of university
          and technical education, major
        . social reforms and advance in
          many other spheres, particularly
          in science and technology.[32]

     The rapid progress of technical and scientific
education is clearly propounded in this message. During
her visit to the U.S., in a recent address at the
National Press Club luncheon, on Friday, 30 July, 1982 she
said that "in all spheres of national activity we have
introduced science and technology as essential tools
for progress."[33]

                       The Faculty

     It is generally admitted that the quality of educa-
tion largely depends on the ability and the devotion
of the faculty. The Education Commission (1964-66) has
emphasized the importance of teachers in the following
words:

          Of all the different factors which
          influence the quality of education
          and its contribution to national
          development, the quality, competence
          and character of teachers are
          undoubtedly the most significant.

                          116

Nothing is more important than
securing a sufficient supply of
high quality recruits to the teaching profession, providing them
with best possible professional
preparation and creating satisfactory conditions of work in which
they can be fully effective.[34]

Siqueira also said that the success of the educational programme largely depends on the character and
ability of the teacher. So the main concern of a college
or university must be to secure an adequate staff with
necessary qualifications for the discharging of its
duties.[35]

Humayun Kabir also stressed the importance of quality
of teachers:

If education trains the future
citizen, it also determines the
shape of future society. The
value of such education depends
on the character and competence
of the teachers who impart it.
That is why the fate of society
depends on the quality of its
teachers. Their incompetence
and dissatisfaction infect the
children and sow the seeds of
revolution and decay.[36]

So the recruitment of persons of high quality in
the teaching staff is very essential in colleges and
universities. The quality of teachers affects the
quality of college students who in turn provide the
leaders of a nation.

The Report of the University Education Commission
(1948-49) emphasised the importance of the teacher and
his responsibility thus:

The success of the educational
process depends so much on the
character and ability of the teacher
that in any plan of university
reform the main concern must be
for securing an adequate staff

117

with qualifications necessary
for the discharge of its many
sided duties. . .The primary responsibility of the teacher is to
arouse the interest of the pupil
in the field of study for which
he is responsible. He has not
merely to cover factual information
and the principles and generalisations
which accrue from them, he has
to stimulate the spirit of enquiry
and of criticism, so that minds
may acquire the habit of exercising
independent and unbiased judgement,
and learn to discriminate between
adequate and inadequate, relevant
and irrelevant data, and to avoid
the extremes of haste and indecision
in arriving at conclusions.[37]

From all this it follows that the right kind of
teacher is one who possesses a vivid awareness of his
calling. He not only loves his subject, but also, loves
the students. His success will be measured not in terms
of percentage of passing alone, nor even by the quality
of original contributions to knowledge, "important as
they are, but equally through the quality of life and
character of men and women whom he has taught.[38]

Further, Report of the University Education Commission of 1967 recommended the following, in order to
attract a significant proportion of talented young men
and women to the teaching profession:

1. There should be minimum national
    scales of pay for university, college,
    and school teacher. The existing wide gap
    between the salary scales for school and
    university (or college) teachers should
    be reduced.

2. The conditions of work and service of teachers
    should be improved and be uniform for teachers
    under different managements.

3. Teachers organizations should be encouraged
    and recognized.

4. The training of school teachers should be
   brought within the broad stream of university
   life and the isolation of training institutions from the schools should be established
   in universities.

5. The academic freedom for teachers to pursue
   and publish their studies and researches
   and to speak and write about significant
   national and international issues should
   be protected.[39]

   At the Vice-Chancellors' Conference held in New
Delhi on September, 1967, Mr. Sen, then the Union Minister
of Education, spoke in his address about the few important programmes for teacher's success:

> The first and the foremost point
> which I would place before you
> refers to the teacher. During
> the last ten years, owing princi-
> pally to the initiative taken
> by the University Grants Commission,
> a good deal of efforts has gone
> into improving the economic condition
> of university and college teachers.
> I am striving my best to see that
> the latest scales of pay sanc-
> tioned by Government are adopted
> by all State Governments as early
> as possible.
>
> I feel more concerned on another
> front, namely, our failure to
> enthuse the average teacher to
> create a climate of sustained
> hard work in his institution,
> to cultivate sense of deep commitment
> to pursuit of learning and excel-
> lence and to develop close identifica-
> tion with the interests of students
> entrusted to his care. I know
> of many noble exceptions and I
> am proud of the fact that the
> teachers as a profession are more
> conscientious than many other
> groups. But as a teacher talking
> to other teachers, I feel that

119

this is a matter where a good
deal more has to be done and that
one of the greatest challenges
facing us today is to generate
this enthusiasm, this commitment
and this identification in the
entire teaching community. To
me this is a matter of the greatest
importance and so long as this
weakness remains, I don't think
that any other reform of higher
education is likely to take us
very far.[40]

There are three recognized grades of teachers according to the recommendation of the University Education
Commission: (1) professors (2) readers and (3) lecturers.

In addition, it appears that a fourth grade analo-
gous to the instructor's grade in U.S.A. or assistant
lecturer's grade in the U.K. is required.[41]

The grading of university staff is based on consideration of experience, scholarship, research and
teaching ability. The highest grade, namely that of
professor, should obviously require the presence of all
these at a high level. Normally the professor ought
to be a person who has taught the highest classes for
a number of years, and has established good reputation
for scholarship. He is not merely a narrow specialist
but has wide interest and a broad outlook, so that he
can inspire and stimulate his colleagues in the department and effectively contribute to the solution of
academic problems of the university. He should have
a keen interest in the advancement of knowledge. He
should be in touch with the latest developments in his
branch of studies. Also he should be an active member
of the caravan which is carrying forward the precious
burden of knowledge, and ordinarily he will be about
the age of 45. In the prime of life, mature in judgement
and possessed of well-tested and well considered ideas,
he should fill the role of leader of both teachers and
students, and of head of the department of his branch
of learning.[42]

Regarding the qualifications of the readers the
Commission recommended the following:

The post of Reader, or as it is
known in the U.S.A. an Associate
professor, is intended for one
who is well qualified to act as
the associate of the professor,
a man of learning and research
who is making his mark in the
world of scholarship. He has
not the length of experience of
the professor as he starts in
his appointment when he is about
35 years of age. But he is not
burdened with administrative duties
as the Professor is, and his main
concern is with teaching and investi-
gation. Either he possesses a
research degree or has published
papers embodying the results of
his researches in recognised and
well-established journals. He
keeps abreast of the progress
of his own line of study, and
is capable of guiding research
students.[43]

With regard to the qualifications of the lecturer,
the Commission recommended that the lecturer should be
expected to have a first class academic record and some
teaching experience. He ought to have a genuine dis-
position towards research and scholarship. A lecturer
should ordinarily have started as a research scholar
or fellow who may have completed a thesis. He should
be able to command the respect of his pupils and should
have sympathy and tact. A lecturer will start about
10 years younger than reader.[44]

The post of instructor or fellow should be a tenure
appointment for term of 3 to 5 years. It should be open
only to Masters of Arts, Science, Commerce etc., whose
academic career has been bright and who have a real bent
for scholarship. The fellow will deal with undergraduate and much of his work will be to direct their
studies. He imparts additional instruction and conducts tutorial classes, under the guidance of senior
members of the staff. He is not overburdened with work,
in order to have enough time to pursue his studies and
lay the foundatons of a career of scholarship and research.[45]

121

To sum up, there are three main or common grades of teachers: professor, reader, and lecturer. A professor is expected to have high academic qualifications, 5 to 10 years of experience, scholarly reputation, and the ability to guide research. A reader must have 5 to 10 years of experience either in teaching, research, or writing. A lecturer must have acquired a master's degree and have a first class academic record. Also it is desirable that he should have some teaching experience.

The Univerity Grants Commission pointed out the following regarding the strength of the teaching staff in university departments and university colleges:

During the period 1964-65 to 1966-67, the strength of the teaching staff in university departments and university colleges rose from 13,637 to 14,900. The number of professors increased from 1,085 to 1,401 of readers from 2,069 to 2,320 and of lecturers (including assistant professors and assistant lecturers) from 9,416 to 19,264. The strength of tutors and demonstrators declined from 1,067 to 915. The proportion of lecturers and readers in the total academic staff was almost static at about 69% and 15% respectively, and that of professors increased from 8% to 14%. the overall strength of the teaching staff increased by 9.3% over the last three years.

In affiliated colleges, the strength of the total academic staff rose from 63,483 in 1964-65, to 78,351 in 1966-67, which shows an increase of 23.4%. The number of senior teachers (including principals and heads of departments) increased from 9,095 to 11,095 of lecturers (including assistant lecturers) from 45,389 to 56,164 and of tutors and demonstrators from 8,999 to 11,092. The proportion of senior

teachers, lecturers and tutors
demonstrators in the total academic
staff remained almost static at
14%, 72%, and 14% respectively.

The ratio of junior to senior
posts was about 3:1 in 1966-67
in university departments and
university colleges. The corresponding ratio for affiliated colleges was about 6:1. The overall
staff student ratio changed from
1:17 to 1:18 during the period
under review.[46]

Salaries of the faculty

The salaries of Indian teachers were very low at
the time of independence. Because of the low pay, the
universities in India are finding it hard to retain their
best teachers. The "good old times" when the profession
of teaching attracted those whom no worldly regards could
tempt are no more. In this age of money economy and
profit motives it is not reasonable to expect that
teachers alone would rise above the spirit of the times.
The competition in salaries between the universities
and other agencies such as industry, governments is
taking the best teachers away leaving the staffs poorer,
envious and discontented. It is not surprising that
Indian universities have failed to produce in adequate
numbers teachers commanding fame and respect or investi-
gators who have won international recognition. A few
have indeed achieved eminence, but the fact remains that
average teacher does not enjoy a high reputation.[47]

In India, the salary scales differ from university
to university and from college to college. The scales
of professional and technical teachers differ from those
of other teachers. The scales in the colleges are not
the same as in the universities. So they have different
types of scale for the same type of work. The scales
are lower in the universities of South-Kerala, Madras,
Mysore, and Andhra, and higher in the universities of
Northern India. For example, the ordinary scale of a
professor in Madras University was Rs. 750 to 1,000,
that of a reader, Rs. 400 to 600, and of a lecturer
Rs. 200 to 300. But the scale of a professor in a
northern university was Rs. 800 to 1250, that of reader

Rs. 500 to 800, and of a lecturer, Rs. 250 to 500.[48]

Professors..................	Rs. 900-1,350
Readers....................	Rs. 600- 900
Lecturers..................	Rs. 300- 600
Instructors or Fellows......	Rs. 250
Research Fellows...........	Rs. 250- 500

The Commission also recommended that special professors should be appointed for a definite term not exceeding five years on Rs. 1500 per month. In case of appointments of professors in technical subjects, a personal allowance not exceeding 500 per month could be given. When a teacher does exceptionally good work, his work may be recognised with a special increment within the grade. For people on the maximum of the grade a special personal allowance may be given in recognition of valuable work. "It should be noted that when the existing grades are changed to the proposed ones the present incumbents are not to be automatically promoted but subjected to the scrutiny of Selection Committees."[49]

Because of low salaries of the faculty, and rising of living standard, the economic condition of the teachers have been very unsatisfactory. Soon after the establishment of University Grant Commission in 1953, grants were given universities for improving the condition. The Commission laid down minimum scales of pay for university teachers and provided assistance to universities to raise the minimum scale, suggested by the commission. They have recommended the following salary scales for university teachers under the Second Five Year plan:

Professors..................	Rs. 800-1,250
Readers....................	Rs. 500- 800
Lecturers..................	Rs. 250- 500
University Teacher below the above rank........	Not less than Rs. 150 per month.

124

The increased cost of upgrading
the salaries of teachers in Central
Universities is borne by the Commission, while for the State Universities, the Commission will bear
80% of the increased cost, the
other 20% of being payable by
the State Government or University
concerned. So far, fourteen State
Universities have implemented
the scheme with financial assistance
from the Commission.[50]

The following Fourth Plan scales of pay for the
academic staff, recommended by the University Grants
Commission and accepted by the Central Government, were
adopted in the central universities to go into effect
April 1, 1966:

Professor.................... Rs. 1,100-1,600

Reader...................... Rs. 700-1,250

Lecturer.................... Rs. 400- 950

It was also agreed that one-third of the number
of professors in the universities might be given the
senior scale of Rs. 1,600-1,800. The additional expenditure involved would be met out of the maintenance
grants payable to these universities.[51]

For the improvement of standards and for the maintenance of universities of India, it has been repeatedly
emphasised that the provision of reasonable salaries
and essential benefits and incentive should be given
to the teaching staff. Also it is important to feed
back a significant proportion of talented men and women
into the teaching field from the colleges and universities. The improvement of salary scales helps to maintain the talented young students, and it helps to attract
and retain well-qualified staff.

The Education Commission (1964-
66) noted that as a result of
the work done by the UGC during
last 10 years considerable improvement has been made in regard to
the pay scales of teachers at

125

the university stage. Assistance was provided by the Commission for improving the salary scales of teachers during the Second Plan period. These scales were further revised during the Third Plan, and grants amounting to Rs. 3,14 crores were paid to the universities and colleges for implementing them. The Commission shared 80% of the additional expenditure involved in the case of the universities and 50% in the case of the colleges. For women's colleges, the Commission shared 75% of this expenditure.

Forty-three universities and 705 colleges were assisted under this scheme. No grant was provided to universities which already had scales identical with or better than tose recommended by the Commission. . . . In 1966-67, grants amounting to Rs. 39.24 lakhs were paid to the universities and colleges under the scheme for revision of salary scales of teachers.[59]

As stated in the report of 1964-66, The Commission recommended a further revision of the scales of pay of university and college teachers as indicated below:

(a) **University Departments**

Professor	Rs. 1,100-1,600
Reader	Rs. 700-1,250
Lecturer	Rs. 400- 950

(b) **Undergraduate College**

Principal	Rs.	700-1,100
Lecturer (Senior Scale)	Rs.	400- 800
(Junior Scale)	Rs.	300- 600
Tutor/Demonstrator	Rs.	250- 400

(c)   Postgraduate College

Principal	Rs.	800-1,250 or
	Rs.	1,000-1,500
Reader/Senior Lecturer	Rs.	700-1,100
Lecturer (Senior Scale)	Rs.	400- 800
(Junior Scale)	Rs.	300- 600
Tutor/Demonstrator	Rs.	250- 400

The Government of India accepted these recommendations and decided to give special assistance to State
Governments for implementing the revised scales from
April 1, 1966. The assistance from the Central Government would be limited to 80% of the additional expenditure involved and will be available for a period of
five years. The State Governments are required to meet
20% of the additions expenditure involved and not to
pass on the liability for any portion of it to the manage-
ments of private colleges.[53]

There are three pay scale grades: Grade I,
Professor - Rs. 1,300-1,600; Grade II, Reader - Rs.
800-1,300; and Grade III, Lecturer - Rs. 400-800.
For example a young man with a brilliant academic
record who enters university service at the age of
25 on Rs. 400 deserves, after 24 years of teaching
experience to get Rs. 1,600 when he is 50 years old.

> The service in a university can
> be considered equivalent to class
> I service of the Central Government
> and to All India services only
> if the running pay-scale is introduced.
> . . If we are really interested
> in attracting first-rate men to
> the universities it's high time
> that some concrete steps were
> taken to offer the same, if not
> comparatively better, terms and
> conditions of service in our univer-
> sities.

> It is sometimes argued that the
> introduction of running pay-scale
> would encourage mediocrity and
> discourage the pursuit of excellence

in teaching and research. A closer
look at this proposal would however,
indicate that such fears are unfoun-
ded. In order to provide incentive
to better than the-average teacher,
promotion from Grade III to Grade
II and from Grade II to Grade
I should be made out of turn.
And then there is the selection
grade for rewarding a teacher
of extraordinary merit and/or
a school of international repute.
Similarly, to punish the lazy
and the careless teacher there
are efficiency bars provided at
two stages in the suggested pay-
scale.[54]

Other benefits of faculty

The University Grants Commission has taken the
following steps to provide many benefits to faculty
or teachers.

1. Because of urgent and pressing need for
    suitable residential accommodation for
    teachers in universities and colleges, the
    Commission has given limited aid to the
    universities and colleges for the construc-
    tion of staff quarters and Teachers hostels,
    sharing 50% of the approved expenditure
    on this account. The Commission meets in
    full the cost of staff houses in central
    universities.

2. The Commission considered a proposal for
    the introduction of sabbatical leave in
    universities and colleges, in order to have
    free time for research and writing books,
    field work, etc.

3. Provided financial support to teachers for
    undertaking research and learned work.

4. The Commission continued to give assistance
    to the universities for the publication
    of research work and doctoral theses.

5. Provided financial assistance for the ex-
    change of teachers to invite distinguished
    teachers or experts who have done outstand-
    ing work in their field or specialisation.

6. Provided a plan to encourage foreign travel
    grants to teachers, if universities pay
    50% of the cost.

7. Contributed regularly to retirement fund
    for teachers who retire usually at the age
    of 60, with possible extension to age 63
    and in special cases to age 65.[55]

    To sum up, since the quality of education largely
depends on the devotion and the ability of the faculty
or the teaching staff, staff morale needs to be improved. Better salary, improved conditions of work,
more academic freedom, all these are necessary in-
gredients for building up staff morale. These factors
need to be improved considerably. If a comparison
is made between the 1948-49 and the present recommended
pay scale, one could see an increase of about Rs.
400 for professors, Rs. 200 for readers, and Rs. 100
for lecturers. But, this increase has not been sufficient to keep up with the upsurging economic condition
of the country. To attract the first rate men to
the universities, substantial steps urgently need
to be taken, though it should be admitted that remarkable progress has been made in a short period of 23
years in improving the conditions of the faculty by
better pay and by providing many other benefits such
as sabbatical leaves, financial support in undertaking
research, exchange of teacher, etc.

    In India, the faculty do not enjoy much academic
freedom in teaching or selecting the text books for
the courses they are teaching. Teachers should be
given the freedom to express their opinions on these
aspects, instead of the matter being determined arbi-
trarily by the curriculum committee. There is a need
to make the curriculum more relevant to the life of
Indian men and women to meet the local needs of the
community. The faculty, students and community should
be given a part in planning the curriculum. There
is urgent need in revising the curriculum and in making
enough provisions for inovations, changes and flexibility,
to make it more meaningful to the students.

Each college should have the freedom to conduct its own examinations and grant its own degrees at least up to the bachelor's level. The colleges should, further, have more autonomy to decide on policies and practices regarding the teaching staff, and new courses of study. The faculty should be made an integral part of the administration for planning curriculum and other academic matters of institution of higher learning.

The teacher problem is still one of the greatest that India faces. The problem is not only one of training and recruiting, but also the salaries and amenities of the teachers. There is considerable disparity in pay between teachers of the Central and State Government universities--the Central Government teachers being favoured (through UGC) over the State University teachers. The teachers in private colleges get the worst treatment. The discontent among these various groups of teachers cannot be remedied until this discrimination is removed. An evolvement of a basic scale on an all-India basis might improve the situation to some extent.

Hours of work or teaching load

Of major importance to many teachers is their teaching load or hours of work. It is measured by the number of hours devoted to lecture, tutorial, or seminar work per week. Universities and colleges vary considerably with regard to the hours of work.

The report of the University Education Commission stated the need for defining the teaching load:

> The hours which a teacher should
> be asked to devote to actual teaching
> should be defined, so that the
> load of teaching is evently spread
> and teachers are not condemned
> to the task of serving up a multi-
> plicity of lectures consisting
> of nothing more than a rehearsal
> of text books available to the
> student. No task is more soul-
> killing than the repetition of
> the same set of lectures from
> year to year. But if the teacher

is compelled to give too many
lectures this is inevitable.
Eighteen periods a week including
tutorial classes is the maximum
that any teacher should be required to do. Those who are in
charge of Master's degree classes
and have to guide research students
should have between 12 to 15
periods.

It must be remembered that lecturing
is not the only duty of the teacher.
It is an important duty but to
carry on research is equally important, and to give advice and to
counsel and to participate in
students' activities are no less
important. A teacher must find
time for study, for unless he
keeps his mind alert and in tune
with the advances in his branch
of knowledge he can neither stimulate the minds of his pupils nor
retain the freshness which is
essential to his teaching.[56]

So the average teaching load for the faculty
is eighteen periods (each period one hour duration)
in the undergraduate college and 12 to 15 periods
in graduate school, per week.

In addition to the regular teaching load, most
faculty members perform other responsibilities, such
as research guidance, testing, grading, advising the
students, and other student and faculty activities.

Methods and improvements of teaching

There are four recognized methods of teaching
employed in modern universities both in India and
in western countries. They are: (1) the lecture,
(2) the tutorial (Oxford type), (3) the discussion
method and (4) the seminar. The methods of teaching
vary in different universities. The common method
of teaching is the lecture to which the other teaching
devices are generally regarded as supplementary.
But the tutorial is the distinguishing method of Oxford

and Cambridge. In the Indian universities and colleges the bulk of the teaching in undergraduate is done in lecture methods, mainly because of the low ratio of teachers to students and extreme shortage of independent rooms. However, the discussion method is being gradually introduced, because of its greater efficacy. The seminary method is used in postgraduate or senior degree classes classes in specialized subjects.[57]

Until recently, practically the only known method of teaching in Indian universities and colleges, was lecture method. The attendance at lectures is compulsory for undergraduate students in London, England, the continental and the Indian universities. . ."In most of the Indian universities a maximum limit of 150 is placed on the number of students attending a lecture, as lectures to larger classes are usually ineffective."[58]

The compulsory attendance at lectures had been a point of controversy in the universities. So the university education Commission suggested:

> The best way would be to make
> attendance at lectures optional
> for post-graduate students who
> are sufficiently mature to look
> after their own interests and
> can judge for themselves what
> is beneficial and what is not.
> The younger students have probably
> to udergo compulsion for some
> time to come as a part of the
> university discipline.[59]

This dominant \lecture method of teaching lowers the standard of teaching. There are several other causes that are responsible for the low standard of teaching in universities and colleges. Some of them are as follows:

1. Class-work and the day-to-day progress of
    the students in their courses of study are
    not given any credit in the university examina-
    tion;

2. the sudden change at the university stage
    in the medium of instruction from the regional
    language to English;

132

3. the appointment of college teachers with
   the bare minimum qualifications;

4. the method of teaching being subject-centered
   rather than student-centered;

5. the failure of the colleges to supply the
   cultural background lacking in the home
   of students coming from the poorer home,
   or belonging to families none of whose other
   members has been educated in a college or
   school;

6. the failure to inculcate the reading habit
   in the students.[60]

In order to improve this low standard of teaching,
the University Education Commission has recommended
the following:

1. The number of formal classroom and laboratory
   hours should somewhat reduced. The time
   thus saved should be devoted, under the
   guidance of instructors, to independent
   study, assigned reading, writing of essays,
   solving of problems and small research projects
   in which the student seeks out and learns
   to use independently the books and documents
   he needs.

2. Every effort should be made to build up
   good libraries in universities and colleges.

3. It is most important to emphasize original
   thinking in the study of all subjects and
   to discourage memorizing.

4. There should be a possibility of undergraduates
   coming into occasional contact with senior
   and outstanding teachers, particularly when
   a new subject has to be introduced for the
   first time.

5. The content and quality of lectures in general
   needs to be considerably improved. One
   way of characterizing the level of class
   work is that every one hour of instruction
   should receive about 3-4 hours of study-
   time to digest lectures.

6. It may be laid down as a rule that no teacher should be away from his institution during 'term time' for more than seven days a year.

7. All new appointments should be made during the period of vacation so that teachers join their new posts at the beginning of the academic year. Further, unless there be compelling reasons, no teacher should be permitted to leave an institution to take up another appointment during term time.

8. There is great need for experimentation, especially in two important areas. One such area concerns the manner of handling larger numbers of students without a proportionate increase in education expenditure or the number of faculty members. Another desirable experiment would be to have a certain amount of teaching done by research students and by selected post-graduate students after their first year.

9. The problem of teaching methods in higher education has been relatively neglected. It should be examined by the UGC through a special committee appointed for the purpose. The schools of education should make a special study of the teaching methods, not only at the school stage, but also in the universities and affiliated colleges.

10. In all teaching universities, external examinations should be replaced by a system of internal and continuous evaluation by teachers themselves.

11. In universities with affiliated colleges, a system of internal assessment should supplement the external examination.

12. The University Grants Commission should set up a Central Examination Reform Unit to work in collaboration with the universities. Special units for examination reform should also be set up in some universities who can be persuaded to organize examination reform in a big way.

13. University teachers should be reoriented to adopt the new and improve techniques of evaluation through a large programme of seminars, discussions and workshops.

14. Early measures should be taken to abolish payment of remuneration to examiners, is a first step, the total number of scripts to be examined by any teacher during a year should not exceed 500.[61]

No standard method of instruction is prescribed by the university or the ministry. Though the traditional lecture method is predominant, other techniques such as tutorials, seminars, discussions, conferences recitation, etc., are in use in higher educational institutions. The gradual introduction of these various methods is an indication that some improvement has been made in recent years. This would, undoubtedly, help in raising the teaching standard and in promoting original thinking rather than memorizing.

Academic freedom

Today academic freedom is very significant in the academic world. Varma stated, concerning meaning of academic freedom:

> Academic freedom means that teacher can not be ordered or required to teach something which goes against his conscience or conflicts with his conception of truth. It also implies freedom of teachers to hold and express their views, however radical, within the classroom and outside, provided they are careful to present the alternative views on a problem without confusing teaching with propaganda in favour of their own particular views. A teacher should be free to pursue and publish his studies and research, and speak and write about and participate in debates on important and significant national and international issues. He should receive

135

all possible facilities and encouragement in his work, teaching
and research, even when his views
and approach happen to be different or divergent from those
of the establishment.[62]

Though this fact is generally recognized, it
is not always upheld for various reasons and circumstances. Some professors may abuse the privilege
at times by teaching only that aspect of an economic,
social, or political issue that corresponds to their
personal views. Such a tendency may lead to indoctrina-
tion rather than teaching.[63]

So the first and most important decision in these
matters rests with the faculty. These decisions should
be taken by each teacher that he will present each
major area of study as fully and fairly as possible.
The teacher and the institution should build this
type of performance and reputation. The governing
bodies and administration should support this kind
of academic freedom in institutions of higher learning
in India. "They will come to understand that threats
to academic freedom strike at the heart of the university's mission in society and ultimately impair society
itself."[64]

Inservice programme

The success of the higher educational programme
depends largely on the competence of teachers. A
competent teacher has to be a continuing student because of the rapid advances in various fields of knowledge. For the continuing education of the teachers,
inservice programmes such as summer school, post-graduate
study, workshops, seminars and conference, etc. must
be provided by the universities and colleges. The
University Grants Commission stated the following:

There is a constant need for increasing
opportunities for teachers to
acquaint themselves with current
developments in their respective
fields of work, and modern curricula
and techniques of instruction.
Teachers have to be exposed to
new concepts and developments

136

to enable them to improve their professional competence and effectiveness. The programme of summer institutes and schools, seminars and conferences is intended to acquaint teachers with new concepts, perspectives and methods. This programme has grown in dimension over the years and has been widely welcomed. The Education Commission (1964-66) has described the programme of summer institutes as "a major instrument in the country's effort towards the improvement of science education, in schools and colleges.

Summer institutes and schools are being run in collaboration with the United States Agency for International Development and the National Science Foundation, U.S.A. The National Council of Educational Research and Training, Ministry of Education, has also been cooperating with the Commission in organising summer institutes for school teachers.[65]

Thirty-three summer institutes for college teachers in science subjects were organised form June 8, to July 15, 1966 in collaboration with the Ohio State University Contract Team of the USAID. For conducting these institutes the Commission paid grants amounting to Rs. 16.35 lakhs to the universities. The USAID provided the services of 76 consultants, who worked as the supporting staff of these institutes and also supplied commodities worth of $15,000 on a grant basis. In addition, Rs. 2.79 lakhs worth of books and equipment were locally purchased and given on a grant basis by the USAID. For these summer institutes, the Commission also supplied books worth of Rs. 2.66 lakhs.[66]

Besides summer institutes, the University Grants Commission has been providing assistance to the universities for refresher courses, seminars, academic conferences, symposia, summer schools, etc.

During 1966-67, 310 proposals were received from 50 universities for holding such conferences, seminars, etc. Of these 71 proposals from 41 universities -30 relating to science subjects and 41 to the humanities and social sciences -were accepted by the Commission for 1966-67. Sixty-two proposals were also approved in 1967-68. During 1966-67, the Commission paid grants amounting Rs. 8.93 lakhs to the universities concerned on this account.[67]

Dr. D. S. Kothari, Chairman of the the University Grants Commission, also stressed the importance of in-service programme in his address at the Vice-Chancellor's Conference, held in September, 1967.

A university or college should therefore spare no pains in attracting and retaining in-service teachers of first-rate ability. The conditions of service of teachers and the general climate in our educational institutions should be such as to draw into the teaching profession in a reasonable proportion of the best talent of the younger generation. This feed back of a proportion of the best into the educational system is vital to the health and progress of the system. In this context an important element is provision for adequate facilities to enable teachers to continually improve and enrich their knowledge and scholarship, Summer Institutes, correspondence courses seminars and conferences (national and international) all play a useful role.[68]

In order to provide opportunities to teachers for acquainting themselves with modern development in their respective fields of study, and new techniques of instruction and curricula the university Grants Commission has assisted a number of universities in organising summer schools, seminars, academic conferences and refresher courses. "The response to this programme has been extremely encouraging and it is proposed to expand this as far as possible. During 1964, sixteen summer institutes were organised for college and university teachers and a similar number for secondary school teachers."[69]

To sum up, the university teacher is no longer confined to his own private study or to his own students. With the new concept of wider duties and responsibilities vested upon the Indian universities since independence the duties and responsibilities of university teachers have expanded.

Dongerkery concluded:

> As a citizen of the new India, the university teacher has obligations to the public at large and to State as well as to his students and his university. He has to keep pace with the advance of knowledge in his own and allied fields of study, and for this purpose he has to remain in constant touch with the work of teachers in other universities by meeting them in conferences and seminars, and by travel if necessary. The practice of granting sabbatical or study leave, which prevails in most of the Modern Universities in the West, and is being rapidly introduced in our own universities in India, is intended to keep the teacher in touch with the progress that is being made in his field, from day to day, in different parts of the world.[70]

The Students

The student body is one of the constituencies of universities and colleges, and it is the responsibility

of the universities and colleges to improve their
condition and education. This section of the dissertation deals with the enrollment of students, admission
requirements, students services and welfare, etc.

Student enrollment

There has been a very sharp increase in the number
of students in the institutions of higher learning
in India since independence. The University Grants
Commission describes about it as follows:

> In the first year of independence
> the university population of India
> was nearly 240,000. In 1951-52
> there were over 400,000 students
> in university classes and colleges
> (not including medical and techno-
> logical institutions). It is
> estimated that number today is
> about 750,000. There has been
> a similar growth in number in
> the professional and technical
> courses, though the increase in
> them has been a controlled one.
> This increase in numbers has
> provided many problems. The
> universities have not been able
> to expand their physical facil-
> ities or to increase the number
> of students. The number of univer-
> sity institutions and colleges
> (not including technical, pro-
> fessional and special colleges)
> during the same period was 532
> in 1946-47, 625 in 1941-52, and
> 746. Inevitably there is a very
> real overcrowding in many of the
> colleges expecially in the large
> cities and the already unsatisfac-
> tory situation with regard to
> contact between teachers and students
> has become much worse in many
> places to the growth of a spirit
> of restiveness among students.[71]

Further, the Commission stated that the present
rate of increase of about 50,000 students annually

in the university institutions who are studying in
arts, science and commerce has to be controlled to
some extent in order to allow for improved educational
standards within the limited resources available.[72]

The University Grants Commission for the year
1966-67 reports the student enrollment for the years
1964-67:

> The total enrollment in the univer-
> sities and colleges during 1966-
> 67 was 1,949,012. This represented
> an increase of 220,239 or 12.7%
> over the enrollment in corresponding
> classes in the preceding year.
>
> . . . During the period 1964-65
> to 1966-67, the increase in the
> total student was 420,785. Of
> this maximum increase of 41.9%
> was in science courses. In arts
> the increase was 34.4%, in commerce
> 8.7%, -- in engineering and tech-
> nology 4.1, in medecine 3.7%,
> -- in law 3.1%, in agriculture
> and education 2.1% each, and in
> veterinary science 9.2%. In other
> courses the enrollment declined
> by 0.3%.
>
> At the graduate level the per-
> centage of enrollment decreased
> from 54.7% to 54.1% during this
> period, and that at the postgraduate
> level came down to 5.2 from 5.5
> in 1964-65. The percentage enroll-
> ment at the research level re-
> mained constant at 0.5. However,
> the actual enrollment at the
> graduate, postgraduate, and re-
> search levels increased by 217,946,
> 17,597 and 2,564 respectively.[73]

"The expansion of educational facilities have been
phenomenal. In 1967-68 for every two thousand of
population there were 33 students in higher educational
institutions. Of this student population, about 22
per cent were females."[74]

Admission requirements

Students who have completed their studies in high school for a period of at least ten years, and have passed the secondary school public examination of the university or its equivalent are eligible for admission to a college for pre-university classes. The students start their schooling at the age of six and usually complete high school at the age of fifteen, if they pass every grade or standard successfully.

Admission requirements are more or less uniform for all institutions of higher learning, but it varies according to the location of the college or the university. The following passage gives an overview of admission requirements:

> The minimum requirement for admission to university faculty is a pass in the Secondary School Leaving Certificate examination, or the matriculation, or the matriculation or entrance examination of university. (At the present time only a few universities in India hold entrance examinations). Although holders of the secondary school leaving certificate or the matriculation examination have already the basic qualification for entry, admission is not automatic since in many faculties the numbers of applications frequently exceeds the number of places available, particularly in faculties of medicine and engineering. Selection procedures are more exacting in these faculties, and most institutions require candidate for admission to engineering faculties to have completed the intermediate science with physics, chemistry and biology.[75]

At present, the admission to government and non-government colleges is based on the marks received at the secondary school leaving certificate examination or its equivalent. "Although students are generally admitted to the universities on the basis of performance in the Matriculation Examinations, University faculty members seem concerned that many of the students are not capable of University work.[76]

To raise the standards by preventing over crowded class rooms, the educational authorities have been giving much attention to selective admission. At the conference of State Education Ministers held in August, 1959, it was suggested that "there should be selective admissions to the universities in order to prevent lowering of standards, overcrowding, wastage on account of failures and students' unrest and lack of employment opportunities for graduate."[77]

At the proceedings of the Second State Education Ministers' Conference, it was pointed out that ". . .While restriction of admission to the universities has become an urgent need, steps will have to be taken simultaneously to make secondary education more practical so that it may be a terminal point for the majority of students."[78]

It was also recommended that there should be selective admissions on the basis of objective admission tests. These tests should measure the following aspects of candidates' qualifications:

(1)   his content of knowledge in appropriate subjects,

(2)   his ability to search and compile relevant information,

(3)   his capacity to organize his knowledge and convey his ideas in speech and writing, and

(4)   his skill in annual and technical work.[79]

Until these objective tests are devised, admissions have to be based on the results of qualifying examinations (Public examinations).

Since these recommendations are in the process of implementation, progress in this area seems to be attainable. Thus, educational quality can be improved by preventing overcrowding, wastage and low standards.

Since the demand for higher education is much
larger than the provision that can be made on the
basis of manpower needs, a system of selective admissions
has been adopted by the 1966 University Education
Commission, based on following points of views:

1. the determination of the number of places
   available in an institution in relation
   to teachers and facilities available to
   ensure that standards are maintained at
   an adequate level.

2. prescription of eligibility by the universities, and

3. selection by the institution concerned of
   the best students from amongst those who
   are eligible and seek admission.

The following are the three measures adapted:

(1) While the use of examination marks as a
    major basis for admissions may continue
    until better selection methods are devised,
    their arbitrariness or lack of reliability
    should be compensated, to the extent possible,
    by making due allowance for the socio-economic
    handicaps of students so as to relate selec-
    tion more directly to innate talent. The
    final selection should also take into considera-
    tion of such factors as the school record
    and the proficiency of the student in fields
    not tested in the examination. This is
    especially important in border-line cases.
    In exceptional cases, the universities should
    have the right and courage to suspend the
    rules and give admissions to students whose
    talent has been identified but who may not
    have been able to fulfill the entrance re-
    quirements. The procedure proposed for
    selecting students on the basis of "school
    cluster" for the award of scholarships may
    also be adopted for making admission to
    quality institutions.

(2) Each university should constitute a Board
    of University Admissions to advise the univer-
    sity about all matters relating to admissions.

144

(3)   The University Grants Commission should
      set up a Central Testing Organization for
      the development of appropriate selection
      procedures for different courses of higher
      education.[80]

The student life, services and welfare

The student life in the Indian universities differ
vastly from student life in the universities of United
States of America or the United Kingdom, because
of the differing social and economic conditions in
which the Indian student lives and studies. Also
it is different today from what it was in the ancient
Indian universities, when the mode of life, customs
and ideas of education were altogether different.[81]

> Two other characterictics of student
> life in India distinguish it from
> American campus life. First,
> nearly all students belong to
> a political party. The Students'
> Congress is a branch of the Indian
> National Congress party, and is
> by far the largest group. The
> Students' Federation is a branch
> of the Communist party and makes
> up in activity what it lacks in
> size. It is not uncommon for
> members of this group to remain
> in college as "students" for many
> years. Other smaller parties
> are sometimes represented.
>
> Second, Indian students exercise
> a greater independence in discipline
> than do American students. Most
> institutions have a Student Union
> in which membership is compulsory.
> The union organizes lectures,
> supervises student organizations
> and deals with faculty as the
> representatives of the student
> body. The strike is a universal
> means of attaining objectives
> and realizing demands.[82]

145

The University Education Commission stated about the functions of student unions thus:

1. Each university should decide how its student union will function, as experimentation in this matter is welcome.

2. Membership of the student union should be automatic, but every student should be expected to choose at least one activity organized in the union.

3. The office-bearers should be elected indirectly by the different student societies in the university, those who spend two or more years in the same class being disqualified for the purpose.

4. Joint Committees of teachers and students should be established and fully utilized to ascertain and redress the genuine difficulties of students.

5. The UGC should take initiative in convening and financially supporting an annual conference of representatives of student unions in universities and colleges.[83]

As it has been pointed out before, the Indian students enjoy freedom of association. About it Reddy recently said:

Freedom of association is a function of an institution of higher learning. An institution of higher education is specifically designed to satisfy a definite need "the need to know." When students are permitted to associate themselves freely with others, either within or outside the scope of recognised student organizations, this need to know is truly met. When freedom to associate with others is restricted, satisfaction of needs is likewise restricted and restricted satisfaction of needs leads to frustration and to discontent.[84]

The task of higher education is not only to provide
classrooms, libraries, and teaching staff, but also
to provide housing, health services, and counselling
for students for the improvement of teaching. Programmes
relating to students' welfare have also been receiving
due attention. Grants are being provided for the
construction of hostels, student homes, nonresident
student centres, health centres and hobby work shops.[85]

The Report of the Parliament Committee on National
Policy on Education recommended that it is desirable
to develop programmes of student services and welfare
at all stages. At the university stage, textbook
libraries should be established in all colleges and
university departments. Also provision should be
made for low cost or subsidized cafeterias and essential
health health services. Further, the Report stated:

> In order to create a sense of
> responsibility and to provide
> civic training, students should
> be associated with the management
> of their institutions in a manner
> suited to their age and maturity.
> . .Joint committees of teachers
> and students should be established
> in each university department
> and in every college to serve
> as a forum for the discussion
> and, where possible, for the
> solution of common problems and
> difficulties. Student's associa-
> tions should also be developed
> on proper line.

> The incidents of student unrest
> can be remedied considerably if
> the educational system is transformed,
> strengthened and made more effective
> on the broad lines as indicated.[86]

The student services are not merely a welfare activity but constitute an integral part of education.
These should include orientation for new students,
health services, residential facilities, guidance
and counselling including vocational placement, student
activities and financial aid. The Commission recommended
the following:

147

1. All institutions of higher education should
    organize orientation programmes for new
    students in the beginning of the academic
    year to facilitate adjustment. Each student
    should be assigned to an academic adviser
    who would assist in planning and organizing
    his programme and studies. Every member
    of the teaching faculty should be expected
    to serve as an academic adviser to a group
    of students.

2. Steps should be taken to organize, on a
    high priority basis, adequate health services
    in universities and colleges. Adequate
    provision should also be made for health
    education of students. The UGC may explore
    possibility of organizing health services
    for university teachers and students on
    the lines of the Contributory Health Services
    of the Government of India.

3. Hostel accommodation should be provided
    as soon as possible, for about 25 per cent
    and 50 per cent of the enrollment at the
    undergraduate and postgraduate stages respec-
    tively.

4. Day-Study Centres, with subsidized or low-
    cost cafeterias, should be provided for
    about 25 per cent of the non-resident students.

5. There should be at least one counsellor
    for every thousand students. A combined
    information and employment centre should
    function directly under supervision of the
    dean of students in each university.

6. It is necessary to develop a rich and varied
    programme of co-curricular activities for
    students not only during term-time but also
    during vacations.

7. There should be a full-time dean of students
    welfare for the administration of welfare
    service.[87]

The Education Commission (1964-66) has stated
that major weakness of the existing system of education

is the failure to provide adequately for student welfare.
This is an aspect of higher education which needs
to be improved on a priority basis.

"Programmes of student services and welfare are
an integral part of educational development. An improvement of the conditions in which students live and
work is expected to have salutary influence on the
attitude and academic performance of students.[88]

The problems relating to student welfare and
allied matters were examined by a committee under
the chairmanship of Dr. T. Sen, the then Vice-Chancellor
of Banara Hindu University. Some of the important
observations of the committee are given below:

1. Every institution should ensure sound arrange-
    ment for work and prompt in redressing legiti-
    mate grievances. Every effort should be
    made to remove the causes of discontent
    among the students.

2. As the living conditions exert a powerful
    influence on the character and personality
    of the students, provisions for hostel facili-
    ties for as large a number of students as
    possible should receive high priority in
    any scheme of educational planning.

3. The scheme for assisting universities to
    set up student home, already being imple-
    mented by the University Grants Commission,
    may be extended to cover as large an area
    as possible.

4. An effective health service system is an
    essential programme of student welfare and
    should be introduced.

5. The state should provide financial assistance
    to poor but meritorious students to enable
    them to continue their studies.

6. A properly organised counselling system
    should be introduced in the universities
    and colleges. If this cannot be undertaken
    on a large scale, due to paucity of resources,
    the tutorial system should be improved and
    encouraged.

7. Before affiliation is given to institutions certain physical standards about numbers, library and laboratory facilities, classroom accommodation, etc. should be insisted upon.

8. There should be increasing participation of students in the business of decision making and programmes in which they are involved, so as to avoid the feeling among them that they are not full members of the university community.

9. It should be impressed upon the students that there are certain areas pertaining to the duties and responsibilities of the institutions which cannot be interfered with, for example, courses of study, examinations, academic standards, appointment of teachers, etc.[89]

The report of the committee has been printed and sent to the universities for their consideration. Many of the universities have followed these recommendations of the committee, and they are in effect at present. Dr. Rao, the former Education Minister of India disclosed that Rs. 30 million ($4 million) had been provided this year for the welfare of university students. "Money will be used among other things for setting up new libraries, hostels and recreation centres. A scheme to identify talent in sports and cultural activities for awarding scholarships is also being instituted."[90]

At present, the guidance and counselling service is very meager; there is an urgent need for improvement in this important area. Courses in couselling and guidance need to be introduced in more universities to train more counsellors.

Women's education

Perhaps even more important than the education of men is the education of women for the full development of human resources, the improvement of homes and moulding the character of children. Indian women shared their part during the struggle for independence, when they fought side by side with men. This equal partnership is essential for the improvement of the

country. Since independence, there has been a great
awakening and today more and more women are interested
in going to schools and colleges. "This is evident
from the fact that while in 1950 six million girls
were attending schools, there are approximately 26
million girls in schools now." The increase in the
institutions of higher learning is even more striking.
For while the figure was only 264 in 1901, it now
stands at 240,000.[91]

The Education Commission has given special consideration for the education of women and provided funds
required for its advancement on a priority basis.
The following recommendations show that women education
has been considered on a priority basis:

1. At present, the proportion of women students
   to men students in higher education is 1:4.
   This should be increased to about 1:3 to
   meet the requirements for educated women
   in different fields. For this purpose,
   a programme of scholarships and provision
   of suitable but economical hostel accomodation
   should be developed.

2. At the undergraduate stage, separate colleges
   for women may be established if there is
   a local demand. At the post-graduate level,
   however, there is no justification for separate
   institutions.

3. Women students should have free access to
   courses in arts, humanities, sciences and
   technology. Courses in home science, nursing,
   education and social work need to be developed
   as these have attraction for a large proportion
   of girls. Facilities for advanced training
   in business administration and management
   should also be provided.

4. Research units should be set up in one or
   two universities to deal specifically with
   women's education.[92]

Today, women in Indian universities enjoy all
the privileges of men. They can take all the courses
open to men and are free to select any optional subjects
of study.

The fact that there is only one
university in the whole country
intended solely for women and
that the majority of women students
study, along with men students,
in all the other universities
courses which mostly prepare for
a man's world, is a clear proof,
if proof were needed, that most
women prefer to receive the same
kind of education as men, and
are prepared to compete with men,
not only in the study of cultural
subjects but also in professional
subjects like education, medicine,
law, commerce, dentistry, and
even architecture and engineering.
Not only are they none the worse
for receiving the same kind of
education as their studies and
even in the professions or callings
they may choose to practice.
They are also able to do full
justice to the posts they may
be called upon to occupy in the
judiciary, at the bar, in administration
and even in business houses.⁹³

Thus, the higher education of women has improved
greatly since independence. There is a large female
enrollment in the institutions of higher learning
in professional education in almost all fields of
higher education. For example in 1947 there were
only about six million attending school. But now
more than 26 million. This shows an increase of more
than four times.

The Curriculum

Curriculum means all the experience of the students
in the school or outside the institutions, under the
supervision of higher educational institutions. It
deals with text books, libraries, media of instruction,
examination, academic year, adult education and extra
curricular activities.

After independence there was an urgent need to
improve and upgrade the curricula of higher education

in India. So the education commission reorganized
the curriculum as follows:

1. The combination of subjects permissible
   for the first degree should also be more
   elastic than at present, both in the arts
   and in the sciences. It should not be
   linked too rigidly to the subjects studied
   at school.

2. There should be general, special and honours
   course at the undergraduate stage. Universities which have better facilities should
   only provide for special courses, minimum
   enrollment being prescribed for the general
   (honours) and special courses to economize
   on costs.

3. It is an urgent need to introduce flexibility
   and innovation in the organization of the
   courses for the Master's degree. The curricula should be framed as to provide a general
   broad-based course or intensive training
   in one or two special fields.

4. A student should be expected to work for
   two to three years for a Ph.D. degree which
   should be regarded as the beginning and
   not the climax of the research career of
   the student. During the first year of the
   Ph.D. course, students should attend lectures
   and tutorials of an advance nature to overcome
   inadequacy of preparation at the Master's
   degree stage.

5. Students for the Ph.D. courses should be
   carefully selected, a time-limit being set
   within which a student is expected to submit
   his thesis. There should also be a limit
   on the number of students to be guided by
   a teacher at any given time.

6. The procedure for evaluation of the Ph.D.
   degree should be improved a defence of the
   thesis being considered an essential requirement
   for the degree.

7. Study of a second world language should
   be obligatory for all Ph.D. students and
   compulsory for the Master's degree in certain
   subjects.

8. It would be desirable to institute the degree
   of Doctor of Science as the highest award
   given on the basis of recognized research
   work.

9. Special efforts should be made to promote
   inter-disciplinary studies in universities
   which have adequately staffed departments
   in related subjects. To further this objective[94]
   a broad-based staffing pattern is also needed.

The Government of India also appointed a number
of review committees to examine the existing syllabi
curriculum and facilities for teaching and research
in various subject of study and to make suggestions
for their improvement and modernisation. "A systematic
study of the academic standards prevailing in universities and colleges was undertaken by a committee
appointed by the Commission in August 1961.
The committee has produced a comprehensive report
and has made important suggestions for improvement
of standards.[95]

The text books

In India the selection of text books is decided
by the text books committee of the universities.
Neither teachers, students, nor the public at large
have much to say about the selection of text books.
Regarding this evil practice the University Education
Commission stated the following:

> One of the evils of the present
> method of instruction is that
> it is focused too much on text-
> books. This evil is most pro-
> nounced in the study of the lan-
> guages and therefore it has become
> almost a racket. A text-book
> is prepared with very little of
> effort as it consists of a number
> of pieces selected from different
> authors, a few copy-right pieces
> being included by permission to

prevent the printing of the selec-
tions and then the publisher and
the author do their best to get
the book prescribed by a university or a board. Once the book
is prescribed, the publisher and
the author are assured of a good
return on their investment but
the poor student does not have
fair deal. The standard for use
in the higher education in India.
Under the guidance of an advisory
committee on the selection of
low-priced books set up by the
UK Government, books are brought
out in what is known as the ELBS
Series (English Language Book
Society Series). . .So far some
100 titles have been republished
under the scheme.[96]

Also an agreement has been made in principle
between Ministry of Education and the Pergamon Press
of Oxford. This provides for any organization designated by the Government of India to enter into specific
agreement with the Pergamon Press for adopting and
translating into English or any Indian language any
book printed by the Pergamon Press in the Commonwealth
and International Library. A few organizations have
already designated for this purpose.

It has also been proposed to initiate a similar
scheme of translation and republication of books of
Russian origin. For this purpose an Indo-Soviet Board
of 10 members: 5 Indians and 5 Russians, on the same
basis of the Indo-American Board has been constituted.
This joint Indo-Soviet Board will consider operating
programmes for publication, translation adoptation,
and distribution of the Russian education books in
India. A similar programme has been initiated with
regard to Indian books published in India, for use
in the USSR.

The programmes of republication of chief foreign
textbooks have started and at the same time suitable
measures have been taken to promote and safeguard
the interest of Indian authors. A scheme for the
publication of low-priced editions of Indian authors'

textbooks as well. At present, suitable assistance is given to Indian authors to write or translate textbooks in India. "The procedure for selection of titles is the same as in the case of American or British books. So far, 11 titles have been selected for republication under this scheme.[97]

For publishing or translating books in Indian languages, the Indian Ministry of Education has recently finalized a scheme. Under this scheme, postgraduate fellowships are offered to students taking up translation in regional languages of books written in foreign languages.

> The scheme which will be implemented
> in universities from next academic
> session will offer 100 fellowships
> to first-class post-graduate stu-
> dents. The students who would
> take up the translation work or
> writing original books in regional
> languages will undergo a training
> course in translation before taking
> up the job. Of successful completion
> of the translation work, as will
> be prescribed by the University
> Grants Commission, the fellows
> will be considered for the award
> of M. Phil. degrees. Those who
> write original books in regional
> languages, according to the standards
> laid down by the University Grants
> Commission will also be considered[98]
> for the award of Ph.D. degrees.

The medium of instruction

The medium of instruction is one of the most controversial subjects in the Indian universities since independence. Before independence, English was the medium of instruction in the institutions of higher learning. Many commissions and committees have considered this issue of language problem:

1. The Wardha, or Zakir Hussain Committee (1937)
2. The Committee on Medium of Instruction set up by the Education Ministry under Dr. Tara Chand (1948)

3. The University Education Commission (1949)
4. The Secondary Education Commission (1952-53)
5. The Language Commission (1956)
6. The University Grants Commission (Kunzru Committee, 1957)
7. The Working Group appointed by the University Grants Commission (1959)
8. The Chief Ministers' Conference (1961)
9. The National Integration Conference (1961
10. The Vice-Chancellors' Conference (1962)
11. The National Integration Council (1962)
12. The Education Commission (1964-66)[99]

The medium of instruction in most Indian universities is still English, though a few of them have adopted Hindi or some other regional language as the medium of instruction for under-graduate course. Ever since independence, public participation has been engaged to find a most suitable medium of instruction for Indian universities and colleges. The University Grants Commission comments:

> The University Education (Radakrishnan) Commission favoured the adoption of the regional language, with the option to use the federal language (Hindi) as the medium of University instruction. But fear was pressed by other bodies like the Inter-University Board that unless all universities of India taught in a common language the possibility of interchange of teachers and scholars and the free movement of ideas and possibly the unity of the country itself would be adversely affected. But the adoption of Hindi as the medium of instruction in Universities in regions where it is not the language of the people will naturally involve considerable difficulties. There are also doubts based on practical considerations regarding the wisdom of changing the medium of instruction at the University stage from English to an Indian language in the immediate future.

157

> The comparative neglect of English
> on the part of University students
> in recent years has, along with
> some other factors, already adversely
> affected the standards of University
> education to some extent.[100]

The report of Education Commission (1964-66) recommended the following concerning the medium of instruction:

1. The regional languages should be adopted
   as media of education at the university
   stage in phased programme spread over ten
   years.

2. At the earlier stage of the undergraduate
   course, the bulk of the instruction may
   be given through the regional language while
   at the post graduate stage it may be in
   English.

3. In due course, all teachers in higher education should, as far as possible, be bilingual
   and post graduate students should be able
   to follow lectures and use reading materials
   in the regional language as well as in English.

4. The maintenance of college teaching through
   the medium Hindi in the non-Hindi areas
   or of Urdu in any part of the country where
   there is a reasonable number of Urdu-speaking
   students, should be permitted and encouraged.

5. Centres of advanced study should be established
   for the development of all modern Indian
   languages including Urdu.

6. The classical and modern Indian languages
   should be provided as elective subject no
   language being made compulsory subject of
   study at the university stage.

7. Adequate facilities should be provided in
   universities and colleges for the study
   of English. Special units for teaching
   English should be established in universities
   to give a good working knowledge of it to

new entrants by the adoption of modern techniques. It would also be an advantage to
teach some English as part of the elective
subject course in the first year of the
degree course.

8. The teaching of important library language
    other than English should be stressed in
    particular the study of Russian, on a large
    scale.[101]

These recommendations have been accepted by some
of the universities in the country. This was pointed
out by Sen in the address of the Union Minister of
Education at the Vice-Chancellors Conference held
on September 1967, in New Delhi:

> Let me point out that this process
> of change-over has already begun.
> As of today 35 universities in
> the country allow a regional language
> as a medium of examination. In
> nearly 15 universities, the proportion
> of students opting for the regional
> language as a medium at this level
> is 90 per cent or more. In 17
> universities, the regional languages
> can be used as media of education
> at the post graduate stage also.
> It is even more important to realise
> that the pace of this change over
> is quickened by several factors,
> such as, the keenness of the State
> Government to bring this change
> about, the adoption of regional
> languages of administrative proposes
> in the States, the virtual break-
> down of English as a medium of
> education in several situations,
> and pressures from the students
> who generally desire an easy way
> out. It will therefore, be clear
> that a change-over to regional
> languages as media of education
> is not something "new." It is
> a process which has already started,
> is now well underway and whose
> pace is being quickened. It is
> both inescapable and irreversible.[102]

Further, it was stated that this change is in the right direction and has to be welcomed. This reform would raise academic standards of higher education, because it would release the creative energies of the people, spread knowledge to the masses, accelerate the process of modernization, and reduce the gap between the people and the intelligentsia. "It has also had the support of all our great national leaders-Tagore, Gandhiji the Rajaji of earlier days-and has been blessed by the Radhakrishnan commission, the Emotional Integration Committee, the Vice-Chancellors' Conference of 1962 and finally the Education Commission. Dr. K. L. Shrimali announced it as a policy of Government in the Parliament.[103]

Again he said at the Conference that all plans of change-over would have to be guided by the following:

1.   The first is the need for an elastic and gradual approach.

2.   The second is the need to strengthen, side by side with the adoption of regional languages as media, the study of English because it gives the students direct access to the growing knowledge of the world. It is only a close cooperation and collaboration between English and regional languages that can raise standards.

3.   It is also essential to evolve a large programme for the production of the needed literature in Indian languages.

4.   One of the major objectives of higher education[104] is to cut across linguistic barriers.

From the above suggestions and recommendations, one could see that the principle of regional languages as the medium of instruction has been accepted. At present, many universities in India are conducting instruction in the regional languages on the under-graduate level. But the medium of instruction at the graduate and post graduate level in most of the universities and colleges is still English. So the problem of implementing this programme is still a big issue, for example, "over 1,000 students have signed a petition asking the Vice-Chancellor of Madras

University to prevent government colleges switching over to Tamil (a regional language) from English, as the medium of instruction."[103]

To summarize, since independence the medium of instruction has been and still is a great issue. The change-over from English to regional languages has already begun, though there are doubts regarding the wisdom of the change at the graduate and post-graduate level. If there was a common language in India, this switch-over from English to that common language would contribute to the unity of the country. In the present situation (with multiplicity of languages) the use of regional languages, especially in the graduate and post-graduate level, would block the way to unity since there is no common means of interstate communication. Teachers and scholars in each state have to confine themselves to their own little language circle. Moreover, they will eventually be cut off from the rest of the world. Those who want to go for higher studies in other states and other countries will find the situation extremely difficult.

This change-over from English to the regional languages in the institutions of higher learning might not facilitate the advancement of knowledge and quality of education. This is due (to some extent) to the difficulty of getting adequate text books and enough teachers who are proficient in English as well as in the regional language. With English as the medium of instruction, uniformity of higher education and exchange of teachers and students between states and other countries would be more feasible. This would promote the maintenance of international quality and character of higher education. Thus the problem of medium of instruction in regional languages is not yet solved in India, especially in South India.

The academic year

The college or university calendar is issued annually by the university. Though the private colleges do not follow this schedule, they are required to include approximately 200 days or 40 weeks of five school days each in an academic year. Most colleges give a week end holiday, Saturday and Sunday, in addition to the public holidays. The college hours extend from 10 a.m. to 4 p.m. with an hour break for lunch

at noon. "The standard collegiate period for a lecture
is fifty minutes. The usual number of lectures for
each subject is three or four a week, and the average
load of full-time student is twenty-four lectures
a week."[106]

In the Commonwealth University Year Book, the
following information is given concerning the number
of terms in an academic year:

> The academic year is divided into
> three terms in most universities.
> Some have only two terms. The
> academic year usually begins in
> June or July and ends in March
> or April. In the Jammu branch
> of the Jammu and Kashmir Univer-
> sity and the Roorkee University
> it begins in September and in
> the Punjab University in October.
> The long (Summer) vacation, except
> in these three universities, falls
> between March and July. The dif-
> ference in the terms and vacations
> is mainly due to climatic conditions.
> Most universities have a short
> break of a fortnight to a month
> in October, and another short
> break of ten days to a fortnight
> in December. No vacation courses
> are held in summer to enable students
> to earn credit for attendance.[107]

The Report of the University Education Commission
has recommended that the university session be divided
into three more or less equal terms, each of ten to
eleven weeks' duration. In this schedule two short
vacations of two or three weeks each and one long
vacation of ten to thirteen weeks would be included.
All other casual holidays should be curtailed during
the academic year. "Every college and university
should so arrange its sessional work as to ensure
a minimum number of 180 working days exclusive of
examination days."[108]

Other recommendations of the appointed committee
suggest a uniform academic calendar for all the universities in India:

1. the academic session in each university should start on a date within a specific period, i.e., between the last Monday of June and the first Monday of July,

2. every university should have a minimum of 180 working days, and

3. the number of holidays be cut down as far as possible.

"The Commission is in favour of extending the working time in the institutions and adjusting the workload accordingly. This, the Commission thinks, does not mean working in shifts but implies the staggering of the time table."[109]

Public examination

For many years, there has been growing dissatisfaction about the public examinations conducted by the Indian universities. There is no correlation between the object of teaching and the aims of examination. The heavy burden is laid on memory and does not encourage students to understand and reflect upon the subjects of their study. About it Misra Stated thus:

> Student life is the best life,
> if there is no examination. This
> examination consists at present
> in chewing, swallowing and vomiting
> some selected texts on a particular
> subject and the examination produces
> a number of degree-holders or
> aspirants hankering after a job
> and the job fetches a salary which
> is not adequate for the bare neces-
> sities of life. Ultimately a
> spirit of frustration and discontent
> reigns supreme. The examination
> system is also responsible for
> premature loss of some lives at
> a very tender age. Those who
> can afford, stood to every kind
> of meanness in order to secure
> a safe passport. Apart from adopting
> unfair means in the examination

hall our students loiter from
place to place soon after the
examination is over and try their
best to gain over the examiners
and in most cases they do succeed.
So both the examiners and the
examinees are not free from cor-
ruption.[110]

This kind of examination system has been considered
one of the worst features of Indian higher education.
Students, coached by their teachers, cram the subject
matter just to pass the public examinations. Aware
of this predicament, University Education Commission
said "that tests and examinations should be designed
chiefly with educational ends in view. They should
help in the choice of students, in the counselling
and guidance of students, in measuring their progress,
in diagnosing present conditions and in devising remedial
measures and finally in assessing educational achievement."[111]

With this view in mind the education commission
has recommended several realistic objectives of examinations:

1.   We recommend that a thorough study of the
      scientific methods of educational testing
      and appraisal be undertaken by the Ministry
      of Education, at the universities with a
      view to applying the results of this study
      in Indian educational practice.

2.   The Ministry of Education should have one
      or two experts who are skilled in the prepara-
      tion and use of objective tests and who
      understand the underlying procedures and
      principles, preferably persons who have
      a Doctor's degree in this field. This would
      provide an agency for centrally organized
      research of testing procedures and a place
      where local results in universities might
      be pooled, and from which advice and assis-
      tance could be sought by the universities.

3.   Each university should have permanent full
      time Board of Examiners with a small staff
      of assistants who can do clerical and routine

work. All the members of the Board, which
need not exceed three in number, should
have at least five years' teaching experience
and at least one should be a highly expert
person in the field of testing and statistics.

The two chief functions of the Board of Examiners
would be:

(a) Advising the university or college instructional
     staff concerning techniques in devising
     and constructing objective tests for their
     class examinations and providing criteria
     and material for the periodic revision of
     the curriculum.

(b) Making periodic and thought inspections
     by use of progress tests in affiliated col-
     leges, which should be required to maintain
     certain academic standards in addition to
     the quantitative criteria now required for
     affiliation.

     The teaching staff in the different areas
     of subject-matter, who are thoroughly familiar
     with the materials in the lectures and courses
     would, of course, be responsible for assembling
     the items to be covered by the tests. They
     would have the technical advice of the Board
     of Examiners in constructing the tests and
     in interpreting possible results and deviations.
     The Board would reproduce them in the qualities
     desired, set and give the examinations,
     score them and announce results.

The experts for the testing service could be
found from at least three sources:

(a) Some qualified persons are available at
     the present. The Commission encountered
     some in the course of its visit to the univer-
     sities. More may be available and their
     service should be utilised in this connection.

(b) A group, which would be sufficient to direct
     Examination Boards at all Universities,
     could be developed by intensive preparation
     and seminars over a period of six months.

For this purpose, we might enlist the services of competent experts in field from other countries.

(c) The Goverment of India could also provide scholarships for Indians in American universities and train the requisite number of experts.

4. We would recommend that a battery of psychological and achievement tests be developed for use with higher secondary school students for the final test at the end of twelve years of schooling. This will, together with other relevant information, serve the purpose of an admission examination to the first degree course at the university. The American Council on Education Cooperative Psychological and General Achievement Tests would serve as a model from which to build a satisfactory basis of selection of Indian students. The service is adapted for the twelfth grade. This Commission is now recommending twelve grades as preparatory to college or university work in India.

5. We recommend that set of objective progress tests for guidance and for evaluating classroom progress should also be developed immediately.[112]

Further, the Commission, with help of a committee and a consultant from the U.S.A., has made a study of the question of examinations. It is expected that some reforms will be gradually effected. The consultant, Dr. Benjamin S. Bloom from the U.S.A., has carefully examined and studied the existing examination system in India and has suggested:

The attack on these problems requires the careful selection and formulation of educational purposes, the development of evaluation materials and instruments which can be used in both internal and external assessment, and development of learning experiences and learning material which can be effectively used by university teachers.[113]

166

In order to accomplish this, Bloom suggested the following:

1. Create a small central planning and coordination staff on university standards and examinations.

2. In each subject field released time of about 5 months should be provided for 50-70 major university teachers.

3. Each university would then determine the rate at which it would move towards an over-all examination for each subject.

4. A few selected member of the different groups may be given additional training in evaluation theory and practice and be appointed as members of a central examination unit.[114]

The 1966 University Education Commission stated that attention should be concentrated on three major areas:

1. reduction of dominance of the external examination,

2. the introduction of reforms which would make them more valid and realistic measures of educational achievement, and

3. the adoption of a good system of internal evaluation.[115]

The public examinations, both at the school and university stages should be improved by employing the latest methods and techniques. The time-lag between the holding of the examination and the declaration of results should be reduced in no case should be longer than about eight weeks.

A comprehensive system of internal assessment covering all aspects of a student's growth should be introduced in all educational

167

institutions, and should be used
for improvement as well as for
certifying the achievement of
the student.[116]

The average pass in Indian universities examination
is about 50%. A few universities have an even lower
standard. About the public examination results, the
statistical survey shows the following facts and figures:

During the year 1964, 786,739
candidates appeared for various
post mariculation annual and
supplementary examinations. Of
these, 397,651 candidates passed.
This gives an overall pass percentage of 50.5. The corresponding
figures for the previous year
were: number appeared 925,494,
number passed 429,032 and pass
percentage 50.4 percent.[117]

These figures show a real wastage in education.
It is measured inversely by the percentage of students
who pass degree examination. This pass average of
50 per cent is not at all satisfactory.

There is no scarcity of recommendations and suggestions regarding the external examination system in
India; yet, this is one of the areas in which very
little progress has been made. The necessity of introducing a comprehensive system of internal assessment
has been stressed over and over again. But the truth
is that though there are internal assessments, these
are not taken into account when the final evaluation
is made. The only criterion used is the final external
examination marks. This vital area needs to be considered seriously by the educational leaders of India.
The real aim of education cannot be achieved as long
as the existing system of external examination prevails.

It is interesting to note, however, that some
improvement has been made in the type of questions
used in the public examination. Until recently, all
questions were essay type; now the questions include
a good number of objective type. Since there are
no standardized achievement tests or entrance examination
to use as criteria for admission, some external exam-

inations could be retained, provided the destiny of students does not depend solely on them.

The libraries

An up-to-date library is essential to every modern university. It is the central source of the necessary tools for the acquisition and advancement of knowledge.

The systematic organization of the American university libraries has evoked the admiration of teachers and scholars all over the world. For example, "In the great library of Harvard University each professor has his study, and each research student his cubicle, where he can keep the books he constantly needs, and the book-stacks are easily accessible to all readers."[118]

The Harvard library, no doubt, has an ideal arrangement for a university centre and is worth copying by every university and college in India.

In the modern university, the library is the only place that still aspires to university. A university differs from other educational institutions in being a place where learning is as much sought by the students as imparted by the teacher. The student should feel that though he may be tied to a paricular course of study, there are no restrictions on his training beyond it, nor any practical conditions limiting his findings within it. He has come up in the first place to ask his own questions and find his own answers. For this he must rely in the main, on the library.[119]

In speaking about priority, Dr. Kotari said that the first place should go to strengthening of the libraries. The situation in the universities and colleges with regard to the availability of indispensable books and journals is not at all satisfactory, even in the post-graduate institutions.[120]

Because of these deplorable library conditions
in Indian universities and colleges, many provisions
for improvement have been made by the Government of
India. The University Grants Commission has provided
millions of rupees for building libraries, supplying
books and journals and other facilities needed. The
Commission decided to sanction Grants on a per cent
basis to arts, science and commerce colleges, having
prescribed minimum enrollment for establishing textbooks libraries which provide books for deserving
students on long-term loans. A text-book grant of
Rs. 10,000 is given under this scheme to a college
offering undergraduate courses leading to the first
degree and Rs. 15, 000 to a college conducting post
graduate courses. By the end of March, 1967, the
Commission had paid grants amounting to Rs. 72.78
lakhs to 726 colleges for this purpose.[121]

Additional assistance available to the universities
under the India Wheat Loan Educational Exchange Programme of the United States has been provided by the
Commission to improve libraries and laboratories.
This provided approximately $1 million annually for
five years most of which went for the purchase of
scientific equipment and books for the Universities
and a few other institutions. Under this scheme,
equipment and books must necessarily be purchased
in the American market. On an average $300,000 have
been spent on purchase of books and journals. Twenty-
four librarians from Indian Universities were sent
to America for a visit of 8-9 months under the plan.[122]

At present, improved library facilities are available to students in all university teaching departments
and other affilitated colleges in various degrees.
A statistical survey shows the following:

> The total stock of books, periodi-
> cals, etc. in all the libraries
> of the universities and their
> colleges (excluding those affili-
> ated to boards of intermediate
> education and also of institutions
> deemed to be universities) were
> 222 lakhs of which about 53 lakhs
> volumes were in university libraries
> and the balance in the libraries
> of constituent and affiliated

colleges. The corresponding figures
for the previous year were 50
lakhs and 155 lakhs respectively.
Of the total volumes, nearly 200
lakhs were books, 14 lakhs were
periodicals, 2 lakhs were manu-
scripts and 6 lakhs other volumes.

About 21.8 lakhs volumes were
added during the year, 17.4 lakhs
in constituent and affiliated
colleges libraries and 4.4 lakhs
in university libraries. Of the
total number added during the
year, 19 lakhs were books.[123]

Adult education

In India, so far very little has been done to
educate the adult, even though adult illiteracy is
an important problem of India. Of the total population,
only about 30 percent are literate, though some states
like Kerala and Delhi have more than 50 percent literacy.

Adult education is sometimes called "community
education," "continuing education," "part-time education"
and "social education." But in India adult education
is generally related to adult literacy or improving
the education of the adult. For a large country like
India, eradication of mass illiteracy is a serious
and urgent problem. For this programme, abundant
resources and all-out efforts are needed. The documentation officer of Indian Adult Education Association
has recently noted:

Adult Education has, therefore,
a wider scope and much deeper
significance. Broadly, adult
education is to provide knowledge,
develop thinking power and broaden
mental horizon of the adult.
According to Lyman Bryson, adult
education means "all activities
with an educational purpose that
are carried on by people engaged
in the ordinary business of life."
Purposeful effort towards self-
development carried on by an

171

individual in all three aspects
of his life - his work, personal
life and as a citizen - is an
essential ingredient of adult
education. It represents the
deliberate and organised endeavour
by which men and women seek to
grow in knowledge after the period
of formal schooling is over.[124]

In order to liquidate mass illiteracy, it is
essential to implement various programmes of adult
education such as part-time education, evening and
week end classes, correspondence courses, and private
study. The part-time classes have to be organised
for employees in large commercial or industrial enterprises, teachers, and others who cannot attend in
regular hours. The Commission stated thus:

Similarly, teachers students and
educational instutions should
be actively involved in literacy
campaign, especially as a part
of the social or national service
programme. The achievement of
literacy should be sustained by
the provision of attractive trading
materials and library services
to the new literature.

Adult or continuing education
should be developed through facilities for part-time on own-time
education and through the expansion and improvement of library
service, educational broadcasting
and television.[125]

For the improvement of adult education, provision
is made for certain categories of students to appear
at public examinations without attending lectures
at recognised institutions. This is very seldom done
in Indian universities, but among those who do attempt
it are generally found school teachers, others connected
with education, and sometimes women. Another attempt
to encourage adult education is through evening or
weekend colleges for the benefit of full time teachers
and workers who are working in different schools and

colleges, and other institutions. Regarding this, the Commission suggested:

> In the large cities of our country, we may consider the feasibility of establishing institutions of this type in Arts and Science for full time workers. These institutions may have to use some of the buildings of the ordinary colleges, but it must be clearly understood that the staff has to be a separate one, as no teacher can possibly work in the evening in addition to teaching day classes. Not only should the teaching staff be separate but all employees of the evening institutions have to be whole-time, and the college must have an organisation absolutely separate from that of the day institutions. Moreover, it may be necessary to lengthen the duration of the courses for any particular degree at these evening colleges because the student will not be able to follow up the lectures with much of home work as a whole time student is able to do. Thus if the ordinary B.A. and B.Sc. courses are three-year ones for the day students, they should extend to four years for the evening students.[126]

Another program which encourages adult education is the tutorial institution. This usually means that a student goes to a teacher at least once a week for private or personal advise and instruction. In the original tutorial at Oxford one student went alone, but now in India the number of students makes it necessary to give tutelage in small groups. At Cambridge, the tutorial is called "supervision." In India very little tutorial work is done in colleges and universities. It is not really a tutorial but merely another lecture-class, because of the size of the group of twenty or twenty-five. Tutorials cannot be employed successfully in groups of more than six students. In most

colleges and universities there is no attempt whatever
at providing any tutorial guidance. This is a serious
deficiency, and improvement in this area is needed
at a very early date. Attendance at tutorial classes
should be made compulsory, even more so than at
lectures.[127]

Concerning the progress of the evening colleges
in India, the following facts are provided:

> During the year 1963-64, 162
> constituent and affiliated col-
> leges and university teaching
> departments had evening classes
> as compared to 121 in the previous
> year. However, information re-
> quired was available only from
> 142 such institutions . . .Of
> these 142 institutions, 95 had
> courses in general education -
> 84 in Arts and 11 in Science.
> 78 of these had courses in pro-
> fessional education - 44 in Com-
> merce, 22 in Law, 3 in Music and
> Fine Arts and 2 in Education and
> Vocational Guidance.
>
> The total enrollment in these
> 142 institutions was 57,530 con-
> sisting of 55,724 boys and 1806
> girls.[128]

Part-time education is another programme for the
expansion of adult education. The Commission has
recommended that opportunities for part-time education
should be extended widely and should include courses
in science and technology. "By 1986, about a third
of the total enrollment in higher education could
be provided through a system of correspondence courses
and evening colleges.[129]

Dr. Kotari, Chairman of the University Grants
Commission, also stressed the importance of adult
education at the Vice-Chancellors Conference:

> In our system of higher education
> a much greater role than at present
> has to be assigned to non-formal

education, i.e., part-time courses,
correspondence courses, evening
classes and private study by
persons in employment. Facilities
for part-time education consti-
tutes an important part of the
system of education in a developing country. It not only makes
contribution to productivity by
improving the knowledge and skill
of those in employment but it
also helps to reduce the pressure
on facilities for full-time education.[130]

The University of Delhi is the first in India
to start postgraduate correspondence. The effort
began in 1969, with courses in Hindi, English and political
science. A school of correspondence course and continuing education has also been started.[131]

This programme of correspondence courses of Delhi
university has achieved great success. At present,
the university is enrolling and preparing students
for the B.A. (pass) degree examination of the university.
the subjects of study are:

1. English--Compulsory for all students.

2. Hindi--compulsory for those whose mother
    tongue is Hindi or who had studied it for
    the higher secondary or intermediate exam-
    ination.

3. Two of the following elective subjects:
    economic, history, political science; commerce;
    mathematics, and sanskrit.

    The entire syllabus for one paper
    of a subject is suitably divided
    into approximately 30 lessons
    each lesson covering the same
    amount of teaching work as is
    done in one week's period in reg-
    ular class room lectures. Lessons
    are prepared by experienced teachers
    of the university and other top
    ranking scholars and are carefully
    edited.[132]

175

The National Board of Adult Education, in one of recommendations at its meeting held in New Delhi on May 4, 1970, gave a new slogan to the country: "each one, teach one." At its meeting the board expressed appreciation of the work of Mharashtra Government in the field of education and suggested "that the pattern of work it is following should be adopted by other State Governments. The board welcomed the action taken by the Education Ministry to include eradication of illiteracy as an essential item in the National Service Programme for college students.[133]

Another important programme in recent years has been adult education through radio and the printing press. The former Education Minister of India, V.K.R. Rao, at the press conference held in New Delhi on April 28, 1970, said that a university of the air would be set up in India shortly. He explained that this would be full-fledged university with Vice-Chancellor, senate, registrar and other governing bodies. "Its unique characteristic would be that it would be conducted entirely through radio. He felt its possibilities were immense in a country like India with a large population and limited resource." He added that a similar university organized in Britain last year, was a signal success there.[134]

Extra-curricular activities

Extra-curricular activities include all the activities of the studnets outside the class room under the supervision of the universities or colleges. Activities include sports, physical education, clubs, unions, associations, National Fitness Corps Programmes, and the National Service Scheme. Dongerkery wrote on the importance of extra-curricular activities:

> The playing field is a necessary
> adjunct to universities and colleges,
> because games like cricket, football
> and hockey not only provide healthy
> exercise and recreation for the
> students, but help them develop
> qualities of leadership, tact,
> judgement and fair play that will
> stand them in good stead in the
> more important game of life for
> which they are preparing. Debating

literary, scientific, dramatic
and musical societies are other
extra-curricular activities that
play an important part in the
building of the character of the
students and also in training
them for public life.[135]

Human beings are psycho-physical in nature. They
have bodies which obey certain laws of growth. They
must be kept in state of health and physical fitness.
Education of the body by physical exercises, sports
and athletic activities helps to develop qualities
of courage, discipline, fair play and team spirit.
"We can not realise fully our intellectual possibilities
without health and physical vigour. No great nation
can be built without strong physical foundings."[136]

The National Fitness Corps Programme is an integrated, multipurpose programme of physical education for
the schools. This programme has been accepted by
most of the State Governments and Union Territories.

The Ministry of Information and Broadcasting
of India states:

The scheme was initiated by the
Government of India during the
Second Plan period to awaken general awareness among the people
of the need and value of physical
fitness and to arouse their enthusiasm for a higher standard
of physical efficiency and achievement.

The National Physical Efficiency
Drive for 1968-69 was organised
all over the country during November, 1968 to January, 1969. As
against the actual participation
of over 10 lakh persons during
the last year, a participation
target of 16 lakh persons was
laid down for 1968-69.[137]

The encouragement offered to the organisation of
sports has been in the following directions:

177

1. Rendering assistance to the National sports
    organisation (one for each game), on the
    advice of the All India Council of Sports,
    for the purchase of sports equipment, sending
    Indian teams abroad, inviting foreign teams
    to play in India, holding national champion-
    ships, etc.

2. Setting up of Sports Council in the States
    Union Territories.

3. Rendering assistance to State Governments
    and National sports organisations for the
    construction of utility stadia.

4. The National Institute of Sports established
    as Patiala in 1961, has so far trained],343
    coaches. It conducts courses in different
    games under the guidance of experts and
    lays special emphasis on popularising sports
    and games in educational institutions and
    rural areas.[138]

Other National Services Schemes are:

NCC Training is no longer compulsory
in colleges and universities.
Instead, students have to choose
between the NCC and two new schemes
- the National Service Corps (NSC)
and the National Sports (NSC).
This was decided on the recommendation of the Education Commission
and a resolution adopted at the
State Education Ministers' Conference last year.

The former programme will include
physical training, social service,
training in civil defence, community
living and other such projects.
The latter will aim at large-scale
promotion of sports with special
facilities for top-class sportsmen.[139]

The Commission also felt the need for setting up
fraternities to foster good-will among the people
of India and the world. Mutual trust and cooperation

can be fostered between the members of different communities, by not emphasising differences of caste
or creed, community and religion. There is a need
to train the students in the democratic way of life
through the extra-curricular activities. They provide
avenues through which students can participate in
making decisions and carrying out joint undertakings.
The students are encouraged to participate in the
social and cultural activities; they will become alive
to the needs of the society in which they live.

        Participation in such activities also help them
to acquire habits of mutual trust and cooperation,
qualities of fair play, patience, disinterestedness,
and consideration for others. These habits cannot
be acquired in institutions run on authoritarian line
since the lesson of freedom cannot be taught by the
methods of servitude.[140]

FOOTNOTES

[1] India: A Reference Annual, 1969, p. 66.

[2] The Report of the Education Commission, 1964-66, p. 67.

[3] Ministry of Education, Government of India, Educational Activities of the Government of India, p. 113.

[4] Report of the University Grants Commission, 1953-57, p.31.

[5] Report of the University Grants Commission, 1966-67, p.22.

[6] Report of the University Grants Commission, 1953-57, pp.31-32.

[7] Report of the University Education Commission, 1948-49, pp. 129-30.

[8] Ibid., p. 34.

[9] Ibid., p. 142.

[10] Report of the University Education Commission, 1948-49, p. 138.

[11] Ibid., pp. 140-141.

[12] Ibid., p. 144.

[13] Ibid.

[14] Ibid., pp. 147-48.

[15] Report of the Education Commission, 1964-66, pp. 104-105.

[16] University Grants Commission, Centers of Advanced Study in Indian Universities (New Delhi: India, 1967), p. 1.

[17] University Grants Commission, Report for the Year 1966-67, pp. 4-5.

[18] Ibid., pp. 21-22.

[19] Report of the Education Commission, 1964-66, p, 102.

[20] Education in Eighteen Years of Freedom, p. 55.

[21] Ibid., pp. 55-56.

[22] Ibid., p. 57.

[23] Ibid., p. 33.

[24] India News, VIII (February 20, 1970), 3.

[25] Ministry of Information and Broadcasting, India Today: Basic facts, p. 32.

[26] Report of the University Education Commission, 1948-49 pp. 255-56.

[27] Education in Eighteen Years of Freedom, p. 11.

[28] Ibid.

[29] Ibid., p. 33.

[30] Education in Eighteen Years of Freedom, p. 36.

[31] The Hindu (India) Oct. 11, 1970, p. 9.

[32] India News, IX (January 8, 1971), 1.

[33] Mrs. Indira Gandhi, Text of Address, National Press Club, Friday, 30 July, 1982, (Washington, D.C.), p. 2.

[34] University Grants Commission Report, 1966-67, p. 24.

[35] Siqueire, op. cit., p. 263.

[36] Kabir, op. cit., p. 185.

[37] The Report of the University Education Commission, 1948-49, p. 68.

[38] Ibid., p. 69.

[39] Report of the Education Commission, 1964-66, p. 70.

[40] Vice-Chancellors' Conference, September 1967, p.7.

[41] Report of the Education Commission, 1948-1949, p. 72.

[42] Ibid., p. 74.

[43] Ibid.

[44] Ibid., p. 75.

[45]Ibid.

[46]Report of the University Grants Commission, 1966-67, p. 2.

[47]Ibid., pp. 70-71.

[48]Ibid., pp. 73-74.

[49]Ibid., p. 78.

[50]The Report of the University Grants Commission, 1953-57, pp. 12-13.

[51]The Report of the University Grants Commission, 1966-67, p. 10.

[52]Ibid., pp. 24-25.

[53]Ibid., pp. 25-26.

[54]Krishna Mohan, "Teaching English in Indian Universities" The Modern Review, CXXIV-VI (February, 1970), 124.

[55]The Report of the University Grants Commission, 1966-67, pp. 26-29.

[56]The Report of the University Education Commission, 1948-49, p. 81.

[57]Dogerkery, op. cit., pp. 137-138.

[58]Ibid., p. 140.

[59]Report of the University Education Commission, 1948-49 p. 105.

[60]Dongerkery, op. cit., p. 167.

[61]Report of the Education Commission, 1964-66, pp. 96-97.

[62]Varma, op. cit., p. 8.

[63]Roland R. Ronne "Decision Making in the Maintenance of Institutional Integrity" Current Issues in Higher Education (Washington, D.C.: The National Education Assocation of the United States, 1963), p. 177.

[64]Emett B. Fields "Academic Freedom, Responsibility and Tenure" The Academic Administration (Texas: Association of Texas College and Universities, 1967), p. 119.

[65]The Report of the University Grants Commission, 1966-67, p. 14.

[66]Ibid., p. 16.

[67]Ibid., p. 18.

[68]D. S. Kothari, "University and National Development," Vice-Chancellors' Conference, September, 1967, p. 26.

[69]Education in Eighteen Years of Freedom, p. 30.

[70]Dogerkery, op. cit., pp. 118-119.

[71]Report of the University Grants Commission, 1953-57, p. 29.

[72]Ibid., pp. 29-30.

[73]University Grants Commission, Report for the Year 1966-67, pp. 1-2.

[74]India Today: Basic Facts, p. 31.

[75]World Survey of Education, p. 608.

[76]A Report of the Seminars on Examination Reform, Evaluation in Higher Education (New Delhi: New Age Printing Press, 1961), p. 2.

[77]Ministry of Education, Proceedings of the Fifth State Education Minister's Conference (New Delhi: Government Press, 1960), p. 55.

[78]Ibid., p. 6.

[79]Ibid., p. 55.

[80]Report of the University Education Commission, 1964-66 p. 100.

[81]Dongerkery, op. cit., p. 124.

[82]Wood, op. cit., pp. 418-24.

[83] Report of the Education Commission, 1964-66, p. 99.

[84] K. S., V. V. Basivi Reddy, "Students' Freedom of Association" University News, VIII (February, 1970), 13.

[85] Education in Eighteen Years of Freedom, p. 31.

[86] Report of the Education Commission, 1964-66, pp. 72-73.

[87] Ibid., p. 99.

[88] University Grants Commission Report, 1966-67, p. 29.

[89] Ibid., p. 30.

[90] India News, IX (May 8, 1970), 3.

[91] India News, VIII (February 20, 1970), 3.

[92] Report of the Educational Commission, 1964-66, p. 101.

[93] Dongerkery, op. cit., p. 259.

[94] Report of the Education Commission, 1964-66, p. 103.

[95] Education in Eighteen Years of Freedom, p. 30.

[96] Ibid., pp. 36-37.

[97] Ibid., p. 37.

[98] India News, IX (May 8, 1970), 3.

[99] Haggerty, op. cit., pp. 100-101.

[100] Report of the University Grants Commission, 1953-57, pp. 11-12.

[101] Report of the Education Commission, 1964-66, pp. 97-98.

[102] Triguna Sen, Vice-Chancellors' Conference, September 1967, p. 9.

[103] Ibid., pp. 9-10.

[104] Ibid., pp. 10-13.

[105] The Times, Educational Supplement, (August 7, 1970), 8.

[106] Aranha, op. cit., pp. 218-219.

[107] Common Wealth University Year Book, 1968, p. 1547.

[108] The Report of the University Education Commission, 1948-1949, p. 102.

[109] University Grants Commission Report, 1966-67, pp. 42-43.

[110] Sen, op. cit., p. 37.

[111] The Report of the University Education Commission, 1948-49, pp. 239-330.

[112] Ibid., pp. 337-339.

[113] Evaluation in Higher Education, p. 23.

[114] Ibid., pp. 23-24.

[115] Report of the Education Commission, 1964-66, p. 71.

[116] Ibid., p. 72.

[117] Ministry of Education, Education in Universities in India, 1963-64, A statistical Survey (New Delhi, Government of India, 1967), p. 31.

[118] Dongerkery, op. cit., p. 263.

[119] A. N. Jha, "Some Aspects of University Education" Indian Education, Journal of the All-India Federation Education Association, V (December 1965-January, 1966), 20.

[120] University Grants Commission Report, 1966-67, p. 25.

[121] Ibid., p. 36.

[122] Ibid., p. 20.

[123] Education in Universities in India 1963-64, A Statistical Survey, p. 36.

[124] J. L. Sachdeva, "Adult Education in Indian Universities," University News, (August, 1970), 17.

[125] Report of the Education Commission, 1967, pp. 68-69.

[126] Report of the University Education Commission, 1948-49, p. 106.

[127] Ibid., pp. 106-107.

[128] Education in Universities in India 1963-64, p. 87.

[129] Report of the Education Commission, 1964-66, pp. 100-101.

[130] Kotari, op. cit., p. 27.

[131] India News, VIII (June 7, 1968), 7.

[132] Ibid., p. 7.

[133] India News, IX (May 15, 1970), 2.

[134] India News, IX (May 8, 1970), 1.

[135] Dongerkery, op. cit., p. 132.

[136] Report of the University Education Commission, 1948-49, pp. 37-38.

[137] India: A Reference Manual, 1969, p. 76.

[138] Ibid., p. 76.

[139] Ibid., p. 75.

[140] The Report of the University Education Commission, 1948-49, p. 53.

CHAPTER V

SUMMARY AND CONCLUSIONS

Summary

Chapter I provided a brief historical background and development of Indian higher education from the earliest times until the end of British Period in 1947. The different periods included were the Hindu, Buddhist, Mohammedan and the British periods. The study in this field seems to show that there was a well-developed system of higher education in ancient and medieval India.

The role of higher education in India since Independence was the topic of the second chapter. Attention was directed to the general aims and functions of higher education, and the State and Central Government roles in higher education. It was noted that the universities in India are controlled mainly by the states. Though the universities are controlled by the states, they enjoy autonomy in their internal administration. There seems to be consesus among the educators that the aims and education should be defined broadly to include the development of physical, mental, social and spiritual powers.

The third chapter described the general aspects of the organization and administration of higher education in India after Independence. Both external and internal organization and administration were discussed. The external organizational system was discussed under: the central government, the state government, various university education commissions, the University Grants Commission, Five-Year Plans, philanthropic and religious organizations. Internal organization and administration dealt with the organizational structure and administration of the universities. After discussing the various types of universities, the hierarchy of university officers and their duties were presented.

Chapter four was concerned with the educational system of India with special reference to higher education. Educational programmes in various stages of post-secondary education were briefly sketched. Pre-university programmes, three-year degree courses, graduate and post-graduate studies, research, and technical and scientific education were some of the programmes considered. Other aspects such as curriculum, students and faculty, library facilities, adult education, and extracurricular activities, were also discussed. The last chapter was devoted to summary and conclusions.

Conclusions

The importance of higher education in India was recognized in the Hindu, Buddhist, and Moslem periods. Then, during the British period, three modern universities in Bombay, Calcutta, and Madras were established in the year 1857. An examination of recent literature, government documents, and publications reveal revolutionary changes that have occurred in the field of higher education since Independence. The appointment of various University Education Commissions, University Grants Commissions, and the Five-Year Plans were great landmarks in the history of Indian higher education.

Rapid and extensive educational, social and economic changes have affected the nation as a whole, especially in the field of higher education. The country has witnessed a significant expansion of higher education since Independence. This is seen from the rapid increase in the number of universities in thirty-five years of independence, from 19 universities in 1947 to 137 in 1982—Seven times the total at the date of independence. Now the question is: Do we need more universities? Surely more universities are needed in India to meet the needs of the growing student population. Mukerjee states: "We have today in the country one person receiving higher education in every forty of the corresponding age group. The figure for the United Kingdom is about one in twelve, and for the United States one in three. This clearly shows the need for expanding university education in the country."[1]

Quantitative expansion, however, does not insure qualitative improvement. Rather, maintenance of quality becomes more complex as universities increase in numbers. Mukerjee also stressed the difficulty of maintaining the quality in the face of widespread indiscriminate expansion of colleges and universities. As Bhan points out,

> While we can gloat over some of the achievements, we cannot remain oblivious of the problems that have raised their head under the spell of expansionist movement. Also, the emerging needs of our society warrant constant re-thinking so as to perfect the system of higher education in a way that it should be rooted in the genius of our developing norms and nuances.[2]

Since Independence, India has been aware of its many problems, not only in education but also in population growth, food, health, economic and language problems. A radical reconstruction of education has taken place in several areas. The educational system has been transformed in relating it more closely to the life of the people in raising the quality of education at all stages, and in the cultivation of moral and social values. Educational opportunities have been expanded and great emphasis has been placed on the development of science and technology. Attempts have also been made in coordinating and maintaining the standards.

A commendable step taken after Independence was the attempt to provide equal educational opportunity to everyone regardless of colour, creed, race, or language. Consequently, great progress has been made educationally, economically and socially among the classes who were once forgotten groups.

A wider conception of the duties and responsibilities of universities has been recognized: in providing leadership in politics and administration, the professions, industry and commerce; in meeting the increasing demand for every type of higher education: literary, scientific, technical and professional. Considering the host of problems India had to tackle since Independence, it can be said that she has made considerable progress in planning and implementing several reform measures. For example, the areas which have witnessed some progress are: reconstruction of organizational structure, research, scientific and technical education,

189

growth in the number of universities and colleges, and improvement in teacher status. One of the areas which has not witnessed much progress is the examination system. In order to bring about desired results, proper communication needs to be established between the planners and those responsible for implementation. This necessitates the involvement and cooperation of all the personnel in the hierarchical system of education.

However, there is good ground to hope that educational reconstruction in India is being well begun. It is unrealistic to expect that all problems would be solved in such a short time. It can be stated that the foundations of a sound educational policy have been laid. Hence higher education in India has many challenges to be met and many crises to face. Much has been done; more remains to be done.

This book has attempted to give an overall picture of the role higher education has played in India since she obtanied her freedom in 1947. Since some knowledge of the past is necessary to understand the present, an overview of historical background of higher education has also been provided. It is hoped that this book would add to the knowledge of scholars who are engaged in the reconstruction of educational systems in India, and aid the student of international interest.

FOOTNOTES

[1] S. N. Mukerjee, "Qualitative Improvement of Higher Education," Indian Education, VII (December, 1967-January, 1968), 15.

[2] Bhan, op. cit., p. 28.

BIBLIOGRAPHY

Books

Association of Indian Universities. University Handbook India
1981-82. New Delhi: Raja Printers, 1981.

Basu, Anathnath. University Education in India Past and Present.
Calcutta: The Book Emporium Ltd., 1944.

_____. Education in Modern India. Calcutta: Orient Book
Company, 1945.

Bhan, Shri Suraj. "A Decennium of Higher Education." Development
of Education in New India. Ed. by N. B. Sen. New Delhi:
New Book Society of India, 1966.

Chaliha, Parag. "Some Thoughts on College Education." Development of Education in New India. Ed. by N. B. Sen. New
Delhi: New Book Society of India, 1962.

Cormack, Margert. She Who Rides a Peacock. Bombay: Asia Publishing House, 1961.

Cramer, John Francis; Brown, George Stephenson; and Spalding,
William. Contemporary Education. New York: Harcourt,
Brace and World, Inc., 1956.

Dongerkery, S. R. University Education in India. Bombay: P. C.
Manaktala Sons, Private Ltd., 1967.

Fields, Emmett B. "Academic Freedom Responsibility, and Tenure."
The Academic Administrator. Ed. by Humphries, Jack W.
Texas: Texas A&M University, 1968.

Haggerty, William J. Higher and Professional Education in India.
U.S. Department of Health, Education and Welfare, Washington,
D.C.: U.S. Government Printing Office, 1969.

Kabir, Humayun. Education in New India. New York: Harper and
Brothers, 1955.

Laska, John A. Planning and Educational Development. New York:
Teachers College, Columbia University, 1968.

Manikham, Raja B. Missionary Collegiate Education in Madras.
Lancaster, Pennsylvania: Conestoga Publishing Company,
1929.

Mudaliar, Laskshanaswami. _Education in India_. Bombay: Asia
    Publishing House, 1960.

Mukerji, S. N. _History of Education in India (Modern Period)_.
    Baroda: Acharya Book Depot, 1966.

Naik, J. B. _The Role of Government in Indian Education_. Delhi:
    National Council of Educational Research and Training,
    Ministry of Education, 1962.

Noronha, George E. _Backgrounds in the Education of India Girls_.
    Washington, D.C.: The Catholic University Press, 1939.

Renne, Roland R. "Decision Making in the Maintenance of Institu-
    tional Integrity." _Current Issues in Higher Education_.
    Ed. by Smith G. Kerry. Washington, D.C.: Association
    for Higher Education, A Department of the National Education
    Association, 1963.

Sargent, John. _Society, Schools and Progress in India_. London:
    Pergemon Press, 1968.

Sequeira, T. N. _Education in India: History and Problems_.
    45th Ed. Bombay: Oxford University Press, 1952.

Singh, Ranjendra Pal. _Humanism and Education: Nehru's Speeches_.
    Jullunder, Delhi 6: Sterling Publishers Ltd., 1966.

Smith, Anna Tolman. "Education in India." _A Cyclopedia of Educa-
    tion_. Ed. by Paul Monroe. New York: The Macmillan Company,
    Vol. III, 1918.

Thingale, S. M., and Paranjpe, S. A. _Educational Problems and
    Administration in the Bombay State_. Kolhapur: Arya Bhanu
    Press, 1956.

White, Ellen C. _Education_. California: Pacific Press Publishing
    Association, 1942.

Yearbook of the Commonwealth. London: Her Majesty's Stationery
    Office, 1969.

Government Documents and Reports

Aggarwal, J. C. _Major Recommendations of the Education Commission,
    1964-66_. New Delhi: Arya Book Depot, 1966.

Government of India Planning Commission. _The New India_. New
    York: The Macmillan Company, 1958.

194

_____. _A Reference Annual_. Fairidabad: Government of India Press, 1969.

India. _The Report of the University Education Commission, 1948-49_. Delhi: Government of India Printing Press, Vol. 1, 1950.

_____. _The Report of the University Education Commission, 1964-66_. Delhi: National Printing Works, 1967.

_____. _Review of Education in India, 1947-1961_. Delhi: Government of India Printing Press, 1961.

Kothari Commission (Recommendation and Evaluation). Meerat-24: International Publishing House, 1967.

Kothari, D. S. "University and National Development." _Vice-Chancellors' Conference_. New Delhi: 1967.

Ministry of Information and Broadcasting. _India Today: Basic Facts_. New Delhi: Government of India Press, 1970.

_____. _India: A Reference Annual 1980_. New Delhi: Government of India Press, 1981.

_____. _India's Constitution_. New Delhi: Publication Division, Government of India Press, 1969.

Ministry of Education. _Education in Eighteen Years of Freedom_. New Delhi: Government of India Press, 1965.

_____. _Directory of Institutions for Higher Education_. New Delhi: Government of India Press, 1981.

_____. _Education in Universities in India, 1963-64. A Statistical Survey_. New Delhi: Government of India Press, 1967.

_____. _Educational Activities of the Government of India_. New Delhi: Government of India Press, 1963.

_____. _Proceedings of the Fifth State Education Ministers' Conferance_. New Delhi: 1960.

_____. _Report of 1967-68_. New Delhi: Government of India Press, 1968.

_____. _Report of the Committee Members of Parliament on Education, 1967_. New Delhi: Government of India Press, 1967.

National Council of Educational Research and Training. The Indian
Year Book of Education, 1961. New Delhi: Sree Saraswathy
Press Ltd., 1965.

_____. Second All-India Educational Survey. New Delhi:
Indraprastha Press, 1967.

Planning Commission. First Five-Year Plan, 1951-56. New Delhi:
Government of India Press, 1956.

_____. Third Five-Year Plan, 1961-66. New Delhi: Government
of India Press, 1961.

Report of the University Grants Commission, 1953-57. New Delhi:
Government of India Printing Press, 1956.

Report of the University Grants Commission, 1966-67. New Delhi:
Government of India Printing Press, 1967.

University Grants Commission. Centers of Advanced Study in Indian
Universities. New Delhi: Government Printing Press, 1967.

_____. Evaluation in Higher Education: A Report of the
Seminars on Examination Reform. New Delhi: New Age Printing
Press, 1961.

_____. Hand Book of Universities of India. New Delhi:
Government Printing Press, 1964.

_____. Vice-Chancellors' Conference. New Delhi: 1967.

World Survey of Education IV: Higher Education. New York:
United Nations Educational, Scientific and Cultural Organization, 1966.

Articles, Periodicals and Dissertations

Aranha, Sister Marie Antoinette. "Higher Education of Women
in India." Unpublished Doctoral Dissertation, Department
of Education, The Catholic University of America, 1964.

Chaturvedi, Bipula. "Higher Education in India and its Problems."
Unpublished Ph.D. Dissertation, University of Iowa, 1962.

Desai, D. M. "Government and Private Agencies in the Administration
of Higher Education." Education Quarterly (October, 1967), 17.

Educational India. (August, 1967), 66.

Embassy of India. _Weekly India News_, V (July, 1960), 5.

_____. _Weekly India News_, VIII (February, 1970), 3.

_____. _Weekly India News_, IX (May 29, 1970), 1.

_____. _India News_, IX (April 24, 1970), 3.

_____. _India News_, IX (May 8, 1970), 3, 13.

_____. _India News_, VIII (June 7, 1968), 7.

_____. _India News_, IX (May 15, 1970), 1.

_____. _India News_, IV (February 4, 1966), 5.

_____. _India News_, VII (July 5, 1968), 4.

_____. _India News_, IX (January 8, 1971), 1.

Gangulee. "Education in India Since Independence: Progress
    and Problem." _India News_, VIII (February, 1970), 3.

The Hindu (India) (October 11, 1970), 9.

Hinogoani, D. K. "Education in India Before and After Indepen-
    dence." _Educational Forum_, XIX (January, 1955), 217-250.

Inter-University Board of India and Ceylon "University News".
    (February-March, 1964), 1.

Jha, A. N. "Some Aspects of University Education." _Indian Educa-
    tion: Journal of the All-India Federation of Educational
    Association_. (December 1965—January 1966), 181.

Larson, Lewis Jennings. "National Planning and Higher Education
    in India since 1947." Unpublished Ph.D. Dissertation,
    George Peabody College for Teachers, 1964.

Mathai, Samuel. "University Administration." _Education Quarterly_,
    (October, 1967), 11.

Mukerjie, S. N. "Qualitative Improvement of Higher Education."
    Indian Education, VII (December 1967-January 1968), 15.

Mohan, Krishna. "Teaching English in Indian Universities."
    The Modern Review, CXXIV-VI (February, 1970), 124.

Murty, Satchidananda. "University and Good Citizenship." The Educational Quarterly, (June, 1959), 157-158.

Panikkar, K. M. "Indian Higher Education: Growth Since Independence." Times Educational Supplement (August, 1962), 213.

Saehdeva, J. L. "Adult Education in Indian Universities." University News, (August, 1970), 17.

Saldanah, Mary Agnase. "The Widening of Higher Education in India with Special Reference to the Third Five-Year Plan." Unpublished Ph.D. Dissertation, syracuse University, 1957.

Shridevi, Shripati. "The Development of Women's Education in India." Unpublished Ph.D. Dissertation, Columbia University, 1954.

"Student Explosion." The States Fortnightly (July 25, 1970), 14.

Tewari, D. D. "Decentralization in Education," Indian Education: Journal of the All-India Federation of Education Association, VII (March, 1960), 4-19.

The Times, Educational Supplement (August 7, 1970), 8.

University News: Chronicle of Higher Education and Research in India, VIII (February 20, 1970), 3.

University News: Chronicle of Higher Education and Research in India, VIII (June, 1970), 151.

Varma, D. C. "University Autonomy." The Education Quarterly, (October, 1967), 8.

Venkatachala Rao, Sampunji Famiah. "Higher Education in India with Special Reference to Third Five-Year Plan." Unpublished Ph.D. Dissertation, Cornell University, 1963.

Walter, Gladys. "Education of Girls in India Under the Methodist Church." Unpublished Doctoral Dissertation, Columbia University, 1949.

Wood, H. B. "Higher Education in India." Teachers College Record, LV (May, 1954), 418-24.

Wright, Ruth Coldwell. "Freedom's Impact on Higher Education in India." Journal of Higher Education, XXIII (April, 1952), 198-208.

Definition of Terms

Affiliated college: a college outside the territorial
limits of the university which enjoys the
privileges of the university.

Bachelor's honors' degree: a four-year degree course
with special curricula.

Bachelor's "pass" degree: an ordinary three-year
degree course.

Constituent college: a college recognized by the
university and situated within its territorial
limits.

Guru: an ancient Hindu teacher. However, the term
now refers to any teacher.

Intermediate college: comparable to a junior college
in the U.S.A. with a three-year degree course.

Parishads: assemblies of Brahmans learned in the
Vedas and Dharmasutras.

Principal: the head of an Indian college; he is equal
to the president of an American college.

Scheduled class: a backward or low class of Hindus.

Senate: the supreme governing body of an Indian university.

Syndicate: the supreme administrative body and executive
authority of an Indian university.

Vihara: an educational centre during the Buddhist
period.

Vedas: the four sacred Hindu scriptures.